The Optimal Town-Gown Marriage:

Taking Campus-Community Outreach and Engagement to the Next Level

STEPHEN M. GAVAZZI

DEDICATION

To those campus and community partners who wish to be build more harmonious
relationships with one another.

CONTENTS

ACKNOWLEDGMENTS

First and foremost, I wish to thank E. Gordon Gee and Joe Alutto for giving me the chance to take the helm of The Ohio State University at Mansfield when the stakes were the highest for both campus and community, and Joe Steinmetz for providing me with the administrative support to carry out my vision. Second, I wish to acknowledge the friendship, encouragement, and collaborative spirit of two academic colleagues – Mike Fox at Mount Allison University and Jeff Martin at Clemson University – and one accomplished entrepreneur – UIU Link's Kim Griffo – who together jumpstarted my foray into the realm of town-gown relationships. Third and finally, I wish to recognize the ongoing and unequivocal support of my wife Courtney, who calmly and consistently urged me to stay the course throughout my term as the senior administrator of a Big 10 regional campus.

1. INTRODUCTORY REMARKS

"We are a college town. We just don't know it."

Mark Romanchuk

I am indebted to Mark Romanchuk, State Representative from the Second District of Ohio, for most succinctly stating what had become painfully obvious to me within the first six months of having accepted the position of Dean and Director of The Ohio State University at Mansfield. At that time, there was not a single soul in all of Richland County, let alone in the entire state of Ohio, who could coherently describe or define the relationship between the Mansfield campus and the surrounding communities. And while the people who offered descriptions of the linkages between the public sector and North Central State College – the technical school that shares the campus with Ohio State Mansfield – seemed a bit more certain about the vitality and importance of those connections, when pressed, those same individuals resorted to rather vague depictions of workforce development needs being met by the courses offered through that college. Missing was any sort of comprehensible description of mutually beneficial town-gown associations. At best, it seemed that I was dealing with a reluctant (if not outright reclusive) college town.

As you might imagine, this proved to be a rather disappointing realization for me as the brand new senior administrator of a Big 10 university regional campus. After twenty years of prior association with the flagship research institution of Ohio as both a professor and director of a family research center on its main campus in Columbus, and with decades of experience in working with various community partners in the greater Columbus metropolitan area, I had come to believe that the one thing I could count on was the good will and investment of the local community in those goals and objectives that were associated with The Ohio State University.

Parenthetically, nearly everyone in the state of Ohio seemed to claim some sort of kinship with Buckeye Nation –alumni or otherwise – and especially during football season. I had thought that fact alone would count for something in my new campus setting. The contrast between the assumptions I carried into my new position and the reality I discovered upon my arrival, however, created a set of early (and often painful) learning experiences for me. While athletics certainly can be an enabler of goodwill toward an institution of higher learning, for instance, it is not a determining factor when community and economic development outcomes are at stake. This is especially true when there is a perceived or real lack of meaningful involvement between the principal partners.

Instead, throughout the early months of my regional campus work I felt like I was constantly reliving one of my favorite scenes from the movie "Indiana Jones and the Lost Ark." At one point close to the end of the film, Indiana Jones (played by Harrison Ford) is sitting astride a white horse while assuredly if somewhat hurriedly giving directions to his companions. As he finishes someone asks him, "And then what?" To which the hero replies sharply, "I don't know, I'm making this up as I go along!" In essence, it felt as if I was constantly concocting connections between campus and community where previously none had existed.

This book is dedicated to helping campus and community leaders come down off of their white horses (and out of their ivory towers) in order to better understand the complexities of campus-community partnerships that can arise from these sorts of connections and interactions. Most importantly, the reader will come to understand how the twin components of the "town" and the "gown" come *together* to determine the relative health and well-being of relationships between institutions of higher education and the communities in which they are embedded. And in the process of pointing the way toward more optimal town-gown relationship characteristics, the hope is that readers will reduce their tendency to rely on knee-jerk (and oftentimes suboptimal) decision-making processes that will negatively impact the town-gown relationship for years to come.

Following the introductory remarks contained in this first chapter, the second chapter of this book chronicles some of the more critical town-gown opportunities and challenges that I faced in my first five years of work as the senior administrator of a Big 10 regional campus. Next is the third chapter of this book, entitled "*Understanding Campus-Community Relationships*," which reviews the emerging body of scholarly literature on town-gown relationships in order to provide readers with an initial foundation for understanding and explaining campus-community interactions. Many predictable disciplines have been involved in the study of town-gown interactions, including economics, city and regional planning, business, and higher education leadership, to name but a few of the more conspicuous lines of scholarship that are covered within these pages. The main objective of this chapter is to use this literature in order to pose (and help readers begin to answer) one essential question: Is the town-gown glass you are drinking from half empty, or half full?

Because I am both a social scientist who studies marriages and families and a marriage and family therapist, I have come to believe that the scholarly literature on marriages and families can and does provide additional invaluable insights into town-gown relationships beyond the books and articles covered in the third chapter. As a result, chapter 4 of this book, entitled *"Town-Gown Relationships and the Marriage Metaphor,"* covers one of the seminal attempts to develop marital typologies that, in turn, has been used to generate illuminating insights into what happens between campus and community relationships, especially over time. Also covered in this section of the book is a parallel line of scholarship on family dynamics that is thought to provide some additional food for thought about the ways in which universities and municipalities can strike a healthy balance between meeting their idiosyncratic needs and pursuing goals and objectives for the common good. The main objective of this fourth chapter is to offer readers a new set of lenses for observing and making sense of the town-gown relationships they are immersed in at present. As well, case examples are used to flesh out the characteristics that help shape the different town-gown relationship types, with special attention paid to the critical role that leaders play in directing campuses and communities toward more optimal ways of relating to one another.

The fifth chapter of this book, entitled *"Measuring Town-Gown*

Relationships," begins by describing the development of the Optimal College Town Assessment (OCTA), and includes a discussion of the quantitative and qualitative data generated by the pilot studies that have been conducted with university campuses and the communities that surround them. The main objective of chapter 5 is to take away the guesswork that typically accompanies attempts to describe and define town-gown relationships by inviting readers to become more data-driven in their approach.

All of the best data gathering efforts are for naught, however, if the information's reliability and validity is questioned. The sixth chapter of this book, entitled "*The Town-Gown Mobilization Cycle,*" provides readers with a thorough explanation of the steps that must be taken both *before* and *after* the information gathering phase of one's work. For example, efforts must be undertaken prior to any data collection activities to raise awareness about the importance of focusing first on the relationship between campus and community and, second, to build coalitions of partners who will publicize and otherwise take part in the information gathering process. In turn, it is also critical to spell out exactly how the data will be utilized, both in terms of reporting results and designing action plans that will inform next steps in the process of building more vibrant town-gown relationships.

The main objective of this sixth chapter is to underscore the importance of seeing data gathering both as a process and, in turn, as a rather vivid reflection of the town-gown relationship itself. Readers are duly warned here: If you suspect that your campus and community does not currently enjoy an optimal (harmonious) relationship, the mobilization cycle may require your involvement in some more strenuous and protracted activities *before* any sorts of data-gathering activities can commence. With that caution noted, the good news here is that this kind of preliminary hard work will not only help create important baseline data, but will also lay the foundation for much more optimal town-gown relationship development down the road.

The seventh chapter of this book is entitled *"Perspectives on Town Gown Leadership."* As illustrated in the case examples contained in previous sections of this book, without explicit support from both the most senior administrator of the campus and the head of the local municipal government, effective town-gown relationships will always be fraught with difficulties. What's more, campus and community leaders must not only be ardent and overt supporters of each other's organizations, they also must have the right relationship skills to make that partnership work.

A total of eight campus and community leaders (four former university presidents and four municipal administrators) participated in a semi-structured interview that focused on various town-gown topics pulled from the extant literature, and their thoughts and reflections are shared in companion sections of this seventh chapter. What we find is that campus and community leaders forge alliances that are built on mutually beneficial goals and objectives that typically are met through actions that involve a mixture of healing past harms, resolving present conflicts, and generating the necessary vision for forward progress.

Corroborating information is brought to bear on the discussion of what university leaders must do to enhance campus-community interaction. Here, a series of selected quotes from previously published interviews conducted with university presidents are brought into the discussion about the importance of being intentional about town-gown relationships.

The main objective of chapter 7 is to help readers gain insight into the processes by which campus and community leaders both conceptualize their roles and, as a result, take specific actions that are designed to strengthen town-gown relationships. It should become clear to the reader that many of the major points made by the university presidents and city administrators interviewed for purposes of the present book are echoes of previous statements made by many other senior campus administrators.

The eighth chapter of this book is entitled *"Town Gown Leadership in Action."* The main objective of this chapter is to center attention on the development of "intentional leadership" within town-gown relationships, a viewpoint that places primary emphasis on the role that leaders must play in

8

developing campus-community connections. This chapter includes an update of the town-gown relationship that I have been affiliated with as the senior administrator of a Big 10 regional campus, which served as a case example of the devitalized relationship in the fourth chapter.

By bringing readers the most up-to-date information on the town-gown relationship that I influenced most directly, I hope to illustrate the fact that even the most disheartening campus-community relationships can become more functional if enough blood, sweat, and yes even tears are willing to be shed by partners on both sides of the aisle. Said somewhat differently, the development of an optimal town-gown relationship must always be seen as a full contact sport that requires continuous participation and maximum effort on the part of the campus and community leaders.

This eighth chapter also contains a verbatim transcription of an interview on town-gown relationships I conducted with E. Gordon Gee, arguably the most well-known university president in the nation. Having served as president at five different major institutions of higher learning – including two stints at The Ohio State University and West Virginia University – Dr. Gee has built up a wealth of experiences in facilitating campus-community interactions that are unparalleled by any of his contemporaries. His insights regarding town-gown relationships were shared with me as part of a larger effort that he and I have undertaken to co-author a series of articles on land grant universities and their outreach and engagement mission. With his permission, some of the thoughts he shared about the impact that university presidents have on town-gown relationships are included as part of this eighth chapter.

Finally, all of this information is pulled together in the ninth and final chapter of this book, entitled *"The Ten Commandments of Town-Gown Relationships."* These Ten Commandments are a series of statements about what campus *and* community leaders must do *together* in order to build more harmonious town-gown relationships with one another. Offered as a somewhat tongue in cheek set of pious instructions, the hope was to provoke some vigorous discussions about the intentionality of leadership efforts undertaken by university administrators and municipal representatives.

The commandments emerge from and underscore the basic idea that town-gown relationships can and should be reciprocally beneficial, especially when campus and community representatives treat each other as equal partners. Readers likely will find it easy to spot the evidence that supports this notion in all of the chapters leading up to the commandments discussion. As a result, it is assumed that the ten commandments discussed at the end of this book will take on a more emergent tone and hence contain easily recognized qualities to which readers already have been exposed, instead of being presented as the received wisdom of a burning bush that all too suddenly appears in the storyline.

2. WHEN PARTNERSHIPS WORK, THE GROUND MOVES (LITERALLY)

The early morning fog of September 6, 2013 broke into bright sunshine as I made my way toward campus. The sky was now a cloudless bright blue, and would remain so throughout the day. It certainly was a harbinger of good things to come. The groundbreaking ceremony for the new off-campus student housing project was scheduled to begin at 10:00 a.m. that day, to be followed by a series of activities built around the presence of our university president, who would be on hand to preside over the festivities.

This was a joyous occasion that had an almost surreal quality to it. My predecessors had been attempting to facilitate the creation of new student housing opportunities both on-campus and off for decades. And even though I had only been dealing with housing issues for two and a half years at the time of the groundbreaking, there was a "third time is the charm" feeling to the housing effort for me personally, in that I had already gone through two false starts with previous potential builders.

My first opportunity to engage in dialogue about student housing was with a local businessman who owned land very close to campus. While it was positioned next to a walkway we had received as part of a sewer and water easement granted to the City of Mansfield approximately a decade earlier, off-campus housing in that location would have meant students would face about a mile and a half walk or bike ride to our campus. The trek from this site would be longer than the three-quarter mile journey that students presently had to make from Molyet Village, the Ohio State owned student housing on the other side of the campus. However, our strong desire for new residential opportunities would have compelled us to provide lighting and emergency telephone service along that path if student housing was built there. In addition, we also would have worked with the local transit authority to provide additional bus loops to serve the students who would be living in those new residences.

The most positive aspect about this first opportunity was that we had a local businessman who was passionate about working with our campus to provide lodging for our students (as luck would have it, he was an Ohio State alumnus). This offer to build housing for our students ran counter to the generally indifferent attitude that many other individuals in the community had expressed about our housing needs up to that point in time. The major downside, however, was the fact that this particular individual had no previous experience in building student accommodations, and additionally could not bankroll the project on his own. Therefore, he needed to find partners who knew what they were doing on the construction side of the operation, and who could lend financial assistance at the same time. Regrettably, that businessman just couldn't pull it together on both of those fronts, and progress on that proposed project ceased to move forward.

Not long afterwards, a company with enormous experience in student housing surfaced on our radar screens, with the offer to build housing for all four of the Ohio State regional campuses (in addition to Mansfield, there are campuses located in Lima, Marion, and Newark). This organization had previously built student housing on campuses around the United States, and also had many company leaders who were Ohio State alumni. A meeting was hastily arranged with the regional campus deans and senior administrators on the Columbus campus. In that gathering, company representatives discussed their intention to build private housing alongside at least three of the four of the Ohio State regional campuses (the landlocked nature of Newark's campus was a significant impediment to a private housing effort being undertaken). Soon after that first meeting, renderings of building styles were distributed to all parties, and promises were made to work directly with each of the regional deans in order to locate the most ideal building sites for each campus.

Unfortunately, a short time later it was revealed that there was more complexity involved within this offer than had been previously understood. The company was simultaneously attempting to attract Ohio State's attention with regard to the selection of builders for the sophomore housing on the Columbus campus. Each and every time that company contacted Ohio State officials, it was to discuss the possibility of being involved in the Columbus campus project. In turn, all attempts on the part of university personnel to contact the company about next steps in planning for the regional campus student housing projects were met with vague assurances that "plans were being formulated." With the passage of time, it became more and more evident that this was "strike two" in the search for housing.

The third opportunity for student housing seemingly came out of nowhere. I had scheduled a meeting with the local YMCA director in order to discuss the possibility of creating a public-public recreational center partnership on university land that could serve both the campus and the community. The director had invited some administrative staff to the meeting, as well as one of her advisory board members. The topic of campus enrollment came up, as the director was attempting to determine the potential for daily use of the recreational facilities by our students. I led by discussing the recent slippage in our enrollment numbers due to the shrinking pool of local high school graduates, something everyone was aware of through recent front page stories appearing in the local paper (I still cringe when I think about the "ENROLLMENT DECLINE AT OSU-M" headline that had greeted me one day earlier that year). At the same time, I also mentioned the large number of students from farther distances away who languished on waiting lists for the limited housing our university operated (Ohio State's Molyet Village accommodated only 200 students), and expressed the hope that, sooner or later, Ohio State Mansfield would find a responsive partner that would build the off-campus housing we needed to grow.

After all, there was an almost unlimited amount of students from Northeastern Ohio (most prominently including the Cleveland, Akron, and Canton metropolitan areas) who wanted the Ohio State brand, but could not make the commute to Mansfield in a reasonable amount of time. Our waiting lists for the student housing that Ohio State operated typically averaged between 100-125 students, and that figure only included those students who were willing to plunk down the $250 deposit required to be placed on the waiting list.

The more recent growth in interest in attending a regional campus had coincided with the Columbus campus having created significantly more selective admissions criteria, in tandem with the university's desire to increase admissions of both out-of-state and international students on the main campus. In combination, these admissions decisions had shut out many applicants from starting on the main campus of Ohio State, all of whom would have to start at a regional campus in order to eventually transfer to Columbus.

After the meeting regarding recreational facilities with the YMCA concluded, a YMCA board member accompanied me out the door. The gentleman asked me if I knew what he did for a living. I replied that I thought he was an architect for a downtown Mansfield firm. "Yes, that's correct," he replied, "but I am also a partner in a company that builds student housing for universities." He noted that his company had done quite a bit of work both in Ohio and across the country, but typically built student housing under contract with a given university. That could change, he explained further, as he and his partners had been paying attention to the remarks I had been making in local media about our potential for growth, especially if student housing were built close to our campus. Oh yes, he added, he also was an Ohio State alum, and wanted to do something great for the university.

Without fully realizing it at the time, I had found the perfect community partner, and I had done so in a most unanticipated fashion. Plans were made to get together very quickly with his company, and it took only a few meetings to conclude that we all shared the exact same thinking about the situation: Housing was necessary for the campus to expand, and in turn this growth would trigger all sorts of development opportunities that would serve as an economic stimulus to the entire geographic area.

In essence, this particular town-gown partnership was forged as a common bond to bring new vitality to the campus area specifically as well as for Richland County as a whole. And there was relatively little delay in executing this vision. Almost one year to the day after that first conversation with that YMCA board member, we held the official groundbreaking ceremony for the off-campus student housing project. You might well imagine my excitement and enthusiasm that morning, reflected in the following remarks that I made to the crowd of local dignitaries, university officials, technical college representatives, and various community stakeholders on hand for the event:

"We observe today not only the imminent benefit of housing resources coming to our combined institutions of higher learning, and not only a soon-to-be profitable venture for a business ally, but in addition we celebrate a significant and growing campus and community collaborative effort, or if you prefer, we are reveling in an emboldened town-

gown partnership. Today we bear witness to an event that symbolizes an end to business as usual, as well as the beginning of something new— something that signifies both a renewal of the initial pact between our community and our campus, as well as certain changes to the original town-gown compact that results from the revolutionary forces that are reshaping our society.

It is axiomatic to state that the world is a very different place right now, especially when compared to the world of fifty years ago when this campus was first brought forth in Mansfield. Long gone are the days in which a campus can ignore the communities that surround it, and those days in which communities can disregard the colleges and universities within their boundaries are numbered as well. Happily for those of us in Richland County, the recent Mansfield Campus Framework Plan, developed by Ohio State Mansfield and North Central State College in collaboration with various campus and community stakeholders, has yielded the concept of a Campus District. At its core, this Campus District concept articulates the need for a more robust set of town-gown relationships, an array of linkages that are guided and directed by issues that are vital to the mutual development and well-being of both the campus and the community. This housing initiative is but the first example of many, many more new connections to come.

Today it is my hope that we all will pledge our best efforts to support this promise of mutually assured construction. For those of us on campus, let us continue to ask ourselves not what the community can do for us, but what we can do for the cities and towns that surround us. And likewise for our community partners, let similar questions be asked over and over again: what can be done to support the Mansfield campus? How can we treat Ohio State and NCSC as the home team in various business dealings and decisions that concern the growth and development of Mansfield, of Ontario, of Shelby, of Galion, and all of the other communities that together comprise Richland County?

In the end, our efforts as partners will be judged best by the fruits of our combined labor. How many more citizens in North Central Ohio will earn degrees from the Mansfield campus? How many more industries will thrive as the result of our educational efforts? How many more businesses will benefit from our recruitment and retention activities to attract and keep students as future residents and employees? Mark my words, today's groundbreaking ceremony will become the epicenter of a transformation in town-gown relations, signifying a tectonic shift in the working relationship between our campus and our surrounding communities."

The president of the student housing firm was on hand to give a speech that outlined similar aspirations for what this kind of partnership offered to the region. Thankfully, this was a vision also shared by many others who also lent their thoughts that day. Chief among those individuals was Joe Alutto, the former Ohio State Provost who was serving as Interim President of the university at that time. Among his many supportive comments, he highlighted the fact that the ability to attract more students from outside the area boded well for the region as a whole. Students who choose to live somewhere inevitably feel a kinship to that area, and are thus more likely to see themselves as someday living and working there. Dr. Alutto, also the former Dean of the College of Business at Ohio State, went on to underscore how the influx of new students would generate both immediate and longer-term benefits to businesses and industry in the region, especially as newly minted alumni decided to make this area their home.

The mayor of Ontario (on whose municipality the student housing project rested), gave some short yet extremely supportive remarks during the event as well. However, even more important were his words to me immediately after we posed with shovels in hand for the media. Pulling me aside, he apologized for what he thought was too a long a delay in his "getting on board with this project," which I took as a reference to the fact that he and his city council members had put me and my staff through a bit of a gauntlet over the previous several months regarding a water and sewer study that had to be conducted in order to connect the property to existing utilities. In brief, the development of property in Ontario would require linkage to the sewer system owned and operated by the City of Mansfield, and the study was the first step in understanding issues surrounding flow capacity and best routes for tying into the system. He shared that the support of the city of Ontario was now firmly committed regarding access to those utilities, and that I could count on him to do everything within his powers to keep the housing project moving forward.

That certainly was a magnanimous statement from the mayor. As time would later tell, however, the infrastructure demands related to the enhancement of properties surrounding our campus were far from resolved. In the weeks and months ahead, there would still be some intense negotiation of issues surrounding those water and sewer linkages as a precursor for development to occur on other surrounding properties, as well as how sidewalk extensions and roadway improvements would be handled.

For the moment, however, there was cause to celebrate. What had taken me almost three years to bring to fruition, and what had not been accomplished previously despite decades of efforts on the part of my predecessors, was now within our grasp. Our campus was going to get the housing it needed in order to grow, and in turn we had initiated a process that would more closely tie us together with both Mansfield and Ontario. And with the passage of time, it can now be seen that the student housing complex was only the first of a rather significant string of economic development opportunities that would be created for the campus and surrounding communities.

For Better and For Worse

In an interesting way, the groundbreaking was not unlike a marriage ceremony. There were partners that were being brought together that day, there were witnesses on hand, and vows were exchanged that spoke of mutual concern and commitment to the relationship. And similar to the ceremony of marriage, the groundbreaking was only the first step on a very long journey toward satisfaction and fulfillment. After all, the hard work that goes into an enjoyable ceremony is only the forerunner of activities that must be undertaken to create and maintain a mutually gratifying relationship. To wit, if you want a happy marriage, you are going to have to put a great deal of effort into that relationship. Exactly the same can be said of a healthy town-gown partnership. It takes a great deal of ongoing work, plain and simple.

In turn, there is literature from the family science field that speaks to a "dance" that occurs between family members as they work toward a comfortable balance between a sense of independence and a sense of being part of something larger than oneself. In the healthiest families, members can have experiences of being separate from one another while simultaneously feeling as if they remain connected to one another. Similarly, it is asserted here that the most functional town-gown relationships are those that reflect how campuses and communities can pursue both individual and collective goals with one another in simultaneous fashion. In essence, well-being is associated with the degree to which the partners are *interdependent* entities, the optimal middle ground between dependence and independence.

The next two chapters of this book are an elaboration of many of the concepts introduced in this brief account of the development of an off-campus housing project that became part of a larger effort to enhance town-gown partnerships. What follows first is a review of the literature on town-gown relationships, with particular attention paid to the many and varied issues that impact the quality of the interactions that take place between campus and community partners. Immediately next is a chapter that utilizes the metaphors of both marriage and family in order to bring new focus to the ways in which campuses and communities can best relate to one another. Great emphasis is given here to the notion that both sides of the partnership must continually work on the ties that bind them together if they are to remain healthy partners in the dance of town-gown relationships.

3. UNDERSTANDING TOWN-GOWN RELATIONSHIPS

The main objective of this third chapter is to begin the process of providing readers with the tools they need to answer the question: Is the town-gown glass you are drinking from half empty, or half full? Or stated a bit differently, how close to an optimal town-gown relationship are you right now? In order to answer questions about where your campus and community are right now in terms of their interactions with one another, you first have to know a little bit about the history of town-gown relationships as a whole, which is where we begin this chapter.

The half empty versus half full drinking glass is a visual representation that I have used at the beginning of all presentations I have made to date on town-gown relationships. On the one hand, the literature on relationships between campuses and communities can make it appear as if the development and maintenance of town-gown relationships can be a relatively miserable undertaking. Take for example this "half empty glass" quote from a 2006 paper on community engagement by Bruning and colleagues:

> *"Historically, town-gown relations have been a source of difficulty, frustration, and annoyance for both the town and the university."*

On the other hand, others have taken a decidedly more positive viewpoint about the opportunities embedded in campus-community connections. Compare and contrast the previous quote with the following "half full glass" excerpt from Mike Fox's 2014 book on town-gown relationships:

> *"There is an important need to identify common issues and approaches… associated with having the college or university present. Communities without a post-secondary institution simply do not have this as a factor in their galaxy of community issues, wants, needs, and opportunities. Most wish they did!"*

These two quotes could not be more dissimilar, and they paint radically different pictures of the quality of town-gown relationships. The "half empty" viewpoint is borne out of a negative set of attitudes, beliefs, and actions adopted and carried out by campuses and communities that perceive themselves as being disconnected from one another and, as a result, share little if any commitment to each other's well-being. In contrast, the "half full" perspective represents town-gown relationships that are experienced as connected in mutually beneficial ways.

You might find yourself wondering, how can perceptions of relationships between campuses and communities be that different? Adopting an economic viewpoint for a moment (as marital researchers do when they employ a social exchange theoretical perspective), one might suppose that people arrive at conclusions about relationship quality through some sort of cost-benefit analysis, as depicted in Figure 1.

The "half empty" perspective would come from the belief that costs outweigh rewards within the town-gown relationship, where greater emphasis is placed on common problems such as conflict over land use and student misbehavior. In contrast, the "half full" perspective would be generated from the viewpoint that rewards such as greater economic benefits, shared goals designed for mutual advantage, and active partnerships eclipse any and all costs associated with the town-gown relationship.

Figure 1: Cost-Benefit Analysis of Town-Gown Relationships

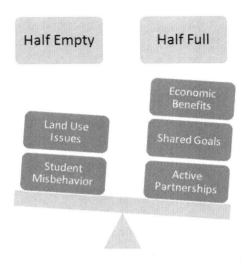

An Historical Perspective

In some very real ways, the "half empty" side of the equation has history on its side. Certain sources of disconnection between town and gown can be traced back to the very birth of universities themselves. Historians provide descriptions of early scholars who took great pains to keep their students shielded from the "immorality" of city life. Medieval university personnel had strong religious affiliations, so these efforts were as much about creating a sense of spiritual separateness as they were about intellectual distinctiveness. As a result, university students slept, ate, and otherwise carried out most of their daily living tasks inside of the university's walls to keep their minds, hearts, and bodies unsullied.

Historical writings further point to a bifurcation of university evolution from the early 1800's forward. In Europe, on the one hand, a number of factors – including most importantly the lack of land immediately adjacent to existing university grounds on which new buildings could be constructed – led to a more complete merging of town and gown sensibilities. In the process of sprinkling college buildings across a wider stretch of land instead of being centralized in a single location, the psychological and physical division between the campus and the community became radically diminished.

On the other hand, more abundant land in America made it possible to erect many new university buildings in one consolidated setting. The widespread adoption of the "campus model" throughout the United States created and maintained demonstrable town-gown divisions. Residences, dining halls, recreational areas and other student life facilities all were built within the confines of the university's property lines. As a result, faculty and other university personnel could continue working in "splendid isolation" from the outside world.

It may seem all the more ironic that this segregation was happening in American communities that contained land grant universities, which were required through the 1862 Morrill Act to provide a range of public services in return for the receipt of federal funding. Of course, 150 years ago the land grant universities largely were expected to focus almost exclusively on the agricultural needs of the community. And to a certain extent, it might be argued that land grant universities continue to do a fairly decent job of meeting these needs today through such mechanisms as extension programs and agricultural research stations.

Contemporary societal needs have grown far beyond the demands of food production, however, and land grant universities have struggled to become relevant in more urbanized settings. Also, various claims have been made that the real problem is that the land grant ideal was lost when the public service began to be seen as an obligatory chore to complete (a box to be checked, if you will) instead of being viewed as part of the need to establish and maintain a vital partnership with the community. Without such dynamic connections, the town-gown relationship – in the land grant context or otherwise – was at risk of becoming both sterile and detached.

Edge/Wedge Issues

The separation of campus and community life is sometimes referred to as the "invisible wall" in the town-gown literature. Continuing with the boundary metaphor for a moment, certain campus "edge" concerns – to wit, what is happening where campus and community meet – often as not become the "wedge" issues that continue to drive the "half empty" perspective. In a 2009 policy report on town-gown collaboration in land use and development, Yesim Sungu-Eryilmaz wrote:

> *"The competing interests of the university, the neighborhood, and the city have three implications. First, even in the era of the engaged university, land use and development processes at the campus edge will repeatedly put town-gown relations to the test. Second, nearly all real estate activities of universities and colleges are multifaceted and have multiple stakeholders, including residents, businesses, and local governments. Third, land uses at the campus edge have become a crucial element in both the physical and socioeconomic character of cities and neighborhoods."*

These "edge/wedge" issues surrounding land use and development typically are accompanied by the perception that the university is encroaching on property in ways that seem to violate the neighborhood or community's identity about itself. And high on the list of common mistakes that aggravate these situations is the university's failure to include local stakeholders in the planning process *before* building activities take place. This sort of relationship blunder inevitably leads to perceptions that the university is at best a paternalistic partner ("we know what's best for you and the neighborhood"). Social justice issues can be needlessly inflamed by this oversight as well, especially if long-term (and oftentimes economically challenged) residents are going to be displaced by university construction activities.

Even when local stakeholders are invited into land use discussions with university personnel, a range of other issues can become contentious rather quickly. For instance, often as not there are "spillover effects" from new construction activities that include everything from new traffic patterns and parking difficulties to upward pressures on rent and other cost of living expenses. Other examples have very real and direct negative consequences for the municipality. There are many situations where land acquisition and subsequent development negatively impacted the property tax situation of a municipality because of the university's nonprofit status. And often as not, university personnel without prior connections to local stakeholders come to the conclusion that it's far less risky to just ride out the storm of criticism about its authoritarian decision-making activities than tempt fate (and induce widespread and very public criticism) by inviting community members to the planning table.

One other "edge/wedge" issue that commands a great deal of attention is centered on student misbehavior, especially regarding those undergraduates who live in off-campus residences. Again, this issue is almost as old as universities themselves. Historians report that incidents of riots and other forms of debauchery connected to "student celebrations" of one sort or another can be found in most every century from the 1400's on.

Although uncommon, some of the more infamous incidents led to murderous rampages, in the process creating victims among students and townspeople alike. These days, the most likely acts of decadence include nuisance behaviors such as intoxication, public urination, and excessive noise. And while not rising to homicidal levels in modern day America, nonetheless this sort of misconduct certainly contributes to the "half empty" perspective on town-gown relationships.

The Glass is Half Full

What then contributes to the "half full" side of the equation? Again we look to historians, who have argued that the rise in importance of medicine and other science-based research efforts within universities helped to create stronger symbiotic relationships between communities and at least certain segments of the campus. University hospitals and other medical facilities have facilitated campus-community connections due to their provision of health care to residents, for example, while science faculty members have contributed empirical assistance to various business and industry sponsors as products and services were developed and tested. Colleges of medicine and engineering in particular continue to expand these sorts of public-private collaborative activities to this day.

Athletics (and particularly successful college teams) certainly have played a role in shifting perceptions toward the "half full" side of the equation as well. In the midst of this book being written, The Ohio State University football team won the first ever College Football Playoff National Championship, and the celebration by "Buckeye Nation" has been widespread. In the process, the euphoria over winning the national title has seemed to heal many of this university's warts (for the time being at least) in the eyes of the community.

In addition to the prestige associated with successful varsity teams in general, there is an enormous amount of money associated with college sports, especially football and basketball. Apart from the substantial television revenue reaped by the universities, there are extensive advertisement opportunities for businesses that associate themselves with these teams. Also, home games create significant economic opportunities for those shops, restaurants, hotels, and other businesses that are located near university stadiums and arenas.

The Land Grant Tradition

The land grant tradition of universities mentioned earlier also has fostered an indelible appreciation for campus-community connections, a stance that bolsters the "half full" viewpoint, at least in theory. From the outset, the Morrill Act that gave rise to the land grant mission of the 19th Century called for universities to serve as regionalized institutions of learning in partnership with the communities that surrounded them. In large part, this meant that each university would shape and, in turn, be shaped by local wishes and desires. This would make every institution of higher learning uniquely qualified to serve the needs of towns and cities in their immediate vicinity, and therefore would become highly prized by community members.

The viewpoint has been expressed repeatedly in the literature that the land grant mission was progressively abandoned by members of the academy over time. As a result, some writers have argued, patronage by community members and financial assistance from state governments for colleges and universities has waned. In at least partial response to this denigration of support, more recent efforts launched during the tail end of the 20th Century have sought to recapture the original sentiments of the land grant enterprise.

Perhaps most auspiciously, this included a series of six reports compiled by the Kellogg Commission on the Future of State and Land-Grant Universities in the mid to late 1990s. Using the theme of "returning to our roots," the Kellogg Commission sought to rethink the role of higher education in American society, with special attention paid to the "engaged institution." From the executive summaries of the report:

> *Embedded in the engagement ideal is a commitment to sharing and reciprocity. By engagement the Commission envisions partnerships, two-way streets*

defined by mutual respect among the partners for what each brings to the table. An institution that responds to these imperatives can properly be called what the Kellogg Commission has come to think of as an "engaged institution."

There were numerous reasons underlying the Kellogg Commission's admonition that state and land grant institutions must assign importance to town-gown partnerships, all of which emphasized the notion that such community connections generally would be of benefit to the campus culture as a whole. That said, one more specific (and highly prized) outcome was the enhancement of the student experience. Recognizing that students serve as one of the "principle engagement resources" available to colleges and universities, their placement in the community as part of their academic activities – especially in service learning efforts – was promoted as an ideal preparatory experience for graduates entering society.

The Kellogg Commission's work directly influenced professional organizations within the higher education realm to explicitly adopt "glass half full" viewpoints in terms of recognizing the value of nurturing healthy town-gown relationships. For instance, the American Association of State Colleges and Universities (AASCU) began advancing a vision of higher education institutions serving as "regional stewards" (also termed "stewards of place") in the early 2000's. Muriel Howard, the AASCU President, provides this description from a 2014 white paper:

"Stewardship is very much a collaboration, with information, resources and ideas flowing back and forth. We share a common destiny. Our institutional success is inextricably linked to the success of our communities, and our communities are the living classrooms and laboratories where our students and faculty learn."

Engagement as stewardship within the AASCU framework became centered on four core areas: development of a more vibrant democracy, partnerships with K-12 schools, fostering community and economic development, and internationalizing communities. Setting their membership apart from flagship and land-grant universities (institutions with futures that were seen as virtually guaranteed), AASCU promoted this four-fold stewardship mission as much for reasons of economic and political survival as it did for the enhancement of the college experience. To wit, institutions that are inextricably tied to the health and well-being of their local communities are likely to garner more public support and thus be in a position to anticipate a more reliable funding stream in the process.

Other organizations followed similar paths in terms of aligning their mission and objectives around the community engagement principles first articulated by the Kellogg Commission. For instance, both the Coalition of Urban Serving Universities (USU) and the Coalition of Urban and Metropolitan Universities (CUMU) have focused on the concept of "anchor institutions." Having first emanated out of a privately funded think tank known as the Anchor Institutions Task Force, the concept of anchor institutions is grounded in the belief that there are a number of select non-profit entities – including colleges and universities, but also hospitals, libraries, museums, community foundations, and the like – that are not inclined to pick up and move geographically. In contrast to the fluid and changing nature of businesses that relocate in the pursuit of more favorable economic climates in which to operate, for instance, these anchor institutions have both the privilege and responsibility of fostering the health and well-being of the communities in which they are located on a more permanent basis.

With the aims and purposes of these higher education organizations as our guide, it seems reasonable to conclude that the pendulum seems to have been swinging decidedly in the direction of the "half full" side of discussions about the nature of town-gown relationships. That said, many of the reasons underlying the "half empty" argument – especially those "wedge/edge" issues described above – continue to place significant challenges in front of campus and community leaders. How these individuals choose to deal with these concerns forms the basis for the relative health and well-being of the town-gown relationship, and is the next topic that this book chapter will explore.

Opportunities and Challenges

If you conduct a Google search using the term "town gown," one of the first references to appear will be a link (www.itga.org) to the International Town and Gown Association (ITGA). ITGA has become the principal organization for individuals who are interested in applied issues regarding how campuses and communities can work together to create more harmonious relationships with one another. The ITGA mission statement reads as follows:

> *The International Town & Gown Association provides a network of resources to assist civic leaders, university officials, faculty, neighborhood residents and students to collaborate on common services, programs, academic research and citizen issues, creating an improved quality of life for all residents, students, visitors, faculty and staff.*

ITGA is concerned predominantly with practical issues that arise at the interface of campuses and communities. As noted above, many higher education-based associations (AASCU, Carnegie, CUMU, Kellogg) have a vested interest in these same sorts of concerns. In addition, more municipally-oriented organizations have paid close attention to applied town-gown issues, including the International City/County Management Association, the Emerging Local Government Leaders, the National League of Cities, and the National Urban League, to name a few of the more active groups.

Town-Gown Best Practices

The main concentration of these associations has been on the application of various "best practices" found in the literature on campus-community relationships. One such example of this kind of work is that of Sungri-Eryilmaz (2009), who directly discussed the best practices that can serve to mitigate the impact of land use issues on town-gown relationships. These strategies include recognition of the need to balance university and community interests, the identification of common town-gown goals, and the commitment to processes and the expenditure of resources that will maximize positive, visible, and long-lasting results. Importantly, Sungri-Eryilmaz underscored the fact that it is difficult if not impossible to devise any sort of "formula" from these strategies that will guarantee satisfaction for all interested parties all of the time. Instead, these practices were offered as general guidelines for creating and maintaining successful town-gown collaborative efforts around land use issues.

Another set of "best practices" were offered by Kemp (2013) in a collection of writings by various authors that describe the ways colleges and universities have formed lasting partnerships within their communities. Within this edited book, a balanced "call to action" regarding new and renewed collaboration activities between campuses and communities on core economic issues was made by Porter and Grogan (2013). On the gown side of things, college and university leaders are implored by these authors to invite community partners into "meaningful participation" in the development of economic development strategies that are designed to be mutually beneficial and sustainable over the long-term. On the town side, mayors and other local government leaders are asked to respond to this open invitation by establishing a liaison office (or at least naming one designated government official) that would serve as the authorized point of contact on all town-gown discussions, as well as building the campus into their own economic development plans. Additionally, business leaders and other community representatives are urged to actively seek out win-win partnerships that would further advance collaborative efforts in areas such as purchasing and supply needs, workforce expansion efforts, and research and incubation activities.

Yet another example of best practices was generated by Bruning and colleagues (2006), who described two paths that lead to strengthened campus-community ties: 1) increasing student access to community resources, often through internships, service learning, and volunteer activities; and 2) linking on issues that speak to the "common destiny" of the campus and community. Of note here is the contention that – when higher education officials do become interested in enhancing town-gown efforts – they typically appear to be one-sided, with resources and people from the campus flowing out into the community. Less prevalent, the authors argued, are active attempts to invite community stakeholders to participate in events or otherwise take advantage of facilities on campus, something their survey research indicated was the key to generating more positive citizen attitudes toward the university. A similar argument has been made by Crawford (2014), who asserted that colleges and universities are important resources that lend themselves quite readily to sustainable communities, including through the sharing of the physical assets of higher education institutions.

By far the most comprehensive work to date on town-gown best practices is that of Michael Fox, much of which is encapsulated in his 2014 book entitled *Town & Gown: From Conflict to Cooperation*. The volume itself is a general primer on all aspects of campus-community relationships, and therefore should be required reading for anyone interested in this area. More specifically, however, is the treatment given to best practices in two critical areas: campus-community relations and community liaison/civic engagement work.

Writing first about best practices in campus-community relations, Fox urged town and gown officials to move beyond the typically reactive relationship that exists between campus and community. All too often, this author cautions, town-gown meetings are called only after a negative event has occurred (usually surrounding student misbehavior of one sort or another).

Instead, a more proactive approach is outlined (in checklist form, no less) as a series of activities that should be taking place by campus and community partners. At a more general macro level, Fox focused a great deal of attention on "studentification," a term originally coined by Darren Smith (2008) to describe issues surrounding the high concentration of college and university students living in close proximity to one another in off-campus housing developments. Higher education administrators and municipal officials alike must share a common understanding of the studentification concerns impacting their community, as well as developing collective strategies for addressing those affairs.

More specifically from the campus side of the equation, Fox implores college and university leaders to take an active role in off-campus issues. Special attention is given to the development of a centralized office for dealing with student housing concerns. When in place, such a department can facilitate the development of policies and procedures for accrediting off-campus student residences, encouraging responsible student behavior in the community through educational programming, and otherwise creating proactive ways to monitor and respond to issues as they arise. In turn, Fox strongly suggested that municipal leaders create various mechanisms for increasing communication outlets on a range of issues of importance to student residents, non-student residents, local government, and campus representatives.

Turning attention to best practices regarding community liaison and civic engagement, Fox highlighted the important role that police and other public safety personnel can play in developing better town-gown relationships. Typically seen as the "heavy hand" in matters concerning student behavior, members of the police force can become a force for good relations through preventative activities that significantly reduce behavioral incidents in the community. Training for police officers on non-confrontational techniques in conflict resolution and the adoption of community policing tactics also can work to greatly reduce negative incidents with students. A variety of non-police partners – including but not limited to firefighters, emergency medical personnel, and government officials that deal with parking, zoning, and by-law enforcement – also were highlighted as playing an effective engagement role with students and university staff and administrators.

In turn, Fox asserted that college and university representatives alike need to wholeheartedly adopt the position of wanting to be a good neighbor by displaying the behaviors of a responsible citizen. Hence, the campus should be represented in town meetings, neighborhood association gatherings, block watches, and as volunteers in various events that target community needs. Additionally, working with police to create party registration services, hosting non-alcoholic festivities, and implementing a comprehensive orientation for students that focuses attention on important town-gown issues are affirmed as going a long way toward the establishment of healthy campus-community interactions.

Table 1: A 4X4 Matrix for Mapping Town-Gown Linkages

	Administration and Staff	Students	Faculty	Governing Board
Business & Industry				
Government & Public Safety				
Local Schools				
Non-Profits, Neighborhood & Social Fabric				

Taken together, these writings strongly suggest that best practices in town-gown relationships are comprised of a number of fairly easily identified steps that campus and community members can take together as partners. To organize information about these connections, a 4X4 matrix is offered to readers in Table 1 above as a heuristic device for assessing the number of town-gown connections that exist in a given locale.

Campus representation exists horizontally across the top of the matrix. In addition to administrators and staff, students, and faculty, the potential impact of members of the governing board that represents the campus is recognized. Whether they are called a board of trustees, regents, or go by some other nomenclature, the members of a college or university governing board can play a critical role in establishing and maintaining effective town-gown relationships. Typically well-connected members of the community – and often as not alumni of the university – governing board members often are selected precisely because they represent the community categories displayed vertically in the matrix rows: business and industry, government, education, and the social fabric (non-profit agencies, community organizations, religious institutions, etc.) of the geographic area served by the campus.

Based on the best practices discussed throughout this section, a greater number of partnership activities across the spectrum of the 4X4 matrix would be equated with increasingly optimal town-town relationships. And perhaps as a minimum standard, an adequate campus-community portfolio might be indicated by the ability to record at least one example of a connection in each of the cells within the matrix.

Summary

The scholarly literature on town-gown relationships was reviewed in order to provide readers with an initial foundation for understanding and explaining campus-community interactions. Historical accounts of universities stretching back to their birth in medieval times provide some support for the "glass is half empty" perspective on town-gown relationships. That is, universities were set up in such a way as to keep the campus and community from interacting in any meaningful way. Further coverage of specific "edge/wedge" issues concerning land use and student misbehavior would seem to generate some additional support for a more pessimistic view regarding town-gown relationships.

On the other hand, knowledge of the many ways that universities have been seen as needing to fulfill an obligation to serve the needs of local communities is a stepping stone toward a more "glass is half full" perspective. The literature concerning best practices in creating and maintaining healthy town-gown relationships also was reviewed, with great attention paid to the ways in which activities undertaken by campus and community representatives promotes a more positive and proactive

approach to the creation of true and lasting partnerships.

4. TOWN-GOWN RELATIONSHIPS AND THE MARRIAGE METAPHOR

The main objective of this fourth chapter is to offer readers a new set

of lenses for observing and making sense of town-gown relationships

through use of the metaphor of marriage. In turn, this section also provides

a blueprint of sorts for moving campuses and communities toward more

optimal ways of relating to one another, with special emphasis on the

documentation of the characteristics and quality of various town-gown

connections.

To introduce the marriage metaphor, it's easiest to begin with a quote

from the paper Mike Fox and I co-authored in 2015 entitled "A Tale of

Three Cities":

What if you had a marriage that was arranged by others, which could not be ended,

but that you had to make work regardless of how you felt about your partner?

That, in a nutshell, is the relationship between a campus and the community that surrounds it. The vows that state "for better or for worse, in sickness and in health," and so on, need never be said out loud between these partners. They are an applied fact of life for any city or town containing an institution of higher education in its midst.

As we stated in that same paper, this is an arranged marriage with no prospect for divorce. However, depending on how well the campus and community partners work with each other, this is a relationship that can range from amazingly productive to outright awful.

Figure 2: The Town-Gown Typology

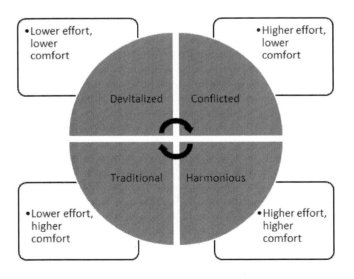

I also co-wrote a conceptual paper in 2014 with both Mike Fox and Jeff Martin that introduced a typology of town-gown relationships as depicted in Figure 2. Borrowing from marital research conducted in the mid-1960's by John Cuber and Peggy Harroff, we advanced the notion that the quality of any relationship was a function of two dimensions – effort and comfort – that together yielded four town-gown relationship types: harmonious, traditional, conflicted, and devitalized. The first two types – harmonious and traditional – tend to be associated with higher satisfaction levels, albeit for very different reasons. The remaining two types – conflicted and devitalized – are connected to lower satisfaction levels, and again with divergent explanations about how they came to be that way.

The Harmonious Town-Gown Type

The most desirable relationship is the harmonious type, which consists of both higher effort and higher comfort levels. Harmonious marriages exist between partners who report elevated satisfaction levels in the midst of engaging in a lot of shared activities with one another. Simply put, the spouses spend a great deal of time together, and in the process enjoy each other's company. In addition, there is the recognition that it takes a great deal of effort to maintain the relatively high quality of this relationship. Therefore, you are only in a harmonious relationship as long as you are willing to do the work!

In a similar way, harmonious town-gown relationships are created when a given campus and community are seen as "getting along" well when they interact with one another. This perception is generated because the town and gown partners are successful in working together across a wide range of undertakings. It is readily apparent that campus and community leaders have established personal connections that seem relaxed and easy going, while recognizing that the only way to maintain such high comfort levels is to continuously expend a significant amount of effort in strengthening the partnership.

The Traditional Town-Gown Type

The traditional relationship type is comprised of lower effort and higher comfort levels. This kind of marriage also has been labeled "passive congenial" by Cuber and Harroff, reflecting the idea that couples of this sort seem to be agreeably disconnected. In a marriage of this sort, partners may be leading separate lives as a result of the relatively small amount of contact they have with one another, either by choice or due to external forces.

The traditional type is the default description for many town-gown relationships. There is a "live and let live" philosophy underlying this type of association. Here, campus and community members tend to ignore each other as they pursue separate goals and objectives. As long as no friction points arise, partners express reserved levels of satisfaction with the relationship. The relatively elevated comfort levels seem to be as much a function of a sense of relief that so little effort is needed to maintain the relationship as anything else.

The Conflicted Town-Gown Type

The conflicted marital type consists of higher effort levels and lower comfort levels. In any healthy partnership, some amount of disagreement is bound to arise, of course. Regrettably, however, partners in conflicted relationships spend rather copious amounts of energy on persistent quarrels that remain unresolved. Cuber and Harroff employed the term "conflict habituated" to signify this sort of ongoing fighting that occurs between spouses. Clearly, these individuals have not (at least yet) given up on the relationship. However, the amount of effort taken up by these enduring struggles is quite demanding, especially if shouting matches are a significant component of how the partners communicate with one another in an ongoing way.

Similarly, the conflicted town-gown relationship often as not reflects a history of unresolved issues from previous struggles. When campus and community representatives are not able to settle their differences on a given issue at one point in time, those individuals (and their successors) can and often do end up fighting those old battles again and again. Over the long haul, these town-gown relationships become caught in a vicious cycle of conflict, even when newly arising issues do not necessarily indicate the need for either side to draw hardline positions. The good news is they haven't stopped trying (representing relatively high effort levels); the bad news is that the partners are increasingly uncomfortable around one another. After all, who wants to fight all of the time?

The Devitalized Town-Gown Type

The fourth and final marital type is the devitalized relationship. Comprised of both low effort and low comfort levels, this is the type of marriage that contains partners who are the least satisfied with one another. Interestingly, devitalized marriages typically are thought to start out as one of the other relationship types, including the harmonious relationship. However, over time a series of injuries have taken place inside of the relationship, resulting in the sense that something valuable was damaged or lost along the way. And while the partners may pine to revisit their glory days, there is little sense of hope that such a return is possible.

The devitalized town-gown relationship similarly can be thought of in terms of disappointment and loss. At some previous point, the campus and the community enjoyed a more positive and promising sense of their future together. For any number of reasons, however, including repeated conflict and unfulfilled promises, the gild has come off of the lily. The town-gown partners are clearly uncomfortable around one another, and they have stopped all efforts to do anything about the relationship.

Town-Gown Types Over Time

Taken together, these four town-gown types offer a way to classify and discuss the nature of campus-community relationships. The harmonious relationship is the most optimal situation, the conflictual relationship is the one that most often creates headaches and headlines, the devitalized relationship is the least desirable condition, and the traditional relationship remains the default arrangement if and when the campus and community can maintain a sense of separation from one another. As noted in the 2014 Gavazzi, Fox, and Martin paper on this subject:

> By default, the traditional modality becomes the preferred state of affairs for most campuses and communities. This town-gown category retains its desirable status if only because it does not take much work to remain embedded in a moderately comfortable relationship. For all intents and purposes, this category might well be labeled the "ignorance is bliss" typology, reflecting a philosophy that lends itself to maintenance of a status quo where town and gown are largely disconnected from one another. However, at the same time this relationship type might just as easily be described as the "nothing ventured, nothing gained" modus operandi. Even further, however, the ongoing stresses and strains that exist on "the edge" of campus properties across the country (especially in more urban locations) make such an

apartheid arrangement near impossible to maintain in practice.

It is important to note that these categories are meant to serve as "snapshots in time" regarding the nature of the town-gown relationship. As such, the levels of effort and comfort experienced between campus and community partners are likely to wax and wane over time, not unlike how marriages and other intimate relationships evolve. The quality of the town-gown relationship is thought to be especially sensitive to changes in management as higher education administrators and municipal leaders come and go. However, any number of other factors also can play a critical role in the altered quality of these associations. Many of these issues – including land use and student behavior – have been introduced in previous sections of this book, and will be revisited and expanded upon in the chapter pertaining to the measurement of town-gown relationships.

Before moving on to some specific case examples that will allow readers to better understand how to apply the typology to specific town-gown relationships, one additional contribution from the marriage and family literature deserves to be introduced here. Research has indicated that the healthiest families maintain appropriate levels of physical and emotional closeness through flexible yet firm interpersonal boundaries. This allows each family member to experience a sense of their own unique individuality alongside the feeling that they are strongly connected to other family members. In comparison, families that are not doing as well tend to err too far in one direction or the other; that is, they either overemphasize closeness at the expense of individuality, or vice versa.

Applying this information to the marital typology, harmonious couples have been able to strike a healthy balance between activities that nurture the relationship and those experiences that support the individual wants and needs of each partner. Stated succinctly, these couples live according to a "fair give and take" principle. In contrast, the other three types (traditional, conflicted, and devitalized) all struggle to find that same equilibrium, with a decided skew toward meeting individual needs at the expense of strengthening the relationship.

Healthy town-gown relationships also seem to follow the fair give and take principle, balancing the achievement of individual goals and objectives with those activities that are mutually beneficial to both campus and community. This is almost the exact description given by several authors who have written about best practices in town-gown relationships. For instance, Sungri-Eryilmaz specifically highlighted the need to identify goals that are shared by campus and community alongside the respect and support of each other's individual interests. Going a bit farther in this line of thinking, McGirr and colleagues discussed how institutions of higher learning needed to remain sensitive to the ways in which individual neighborhoods surrounding the campus might have differentiated needs, thus arguing against a "cookie cutter" approach to community engagement.

Application of the Model

According to the Princeton Review, for the past seven years Clemson University and the City of Clemson have represented the top rated example of great town-gown relationships in the United States. In 2014, I attended the International Town Gown Association conference held at Clemson, and I came away believing wholeheartedly that the highest honors were indeed applicable to this particular campus-community relationship. One quick story from that visit shall suffice here, although there are countless others I could tell.

At the beginning of the conference, the mayor of Clemson – a true southern gentleman named J.C. Cook – gave a brief set of opening remarks to the attendees. Following his short speech, Mayor Cook got off the stage and sat down in the front row. How nice, I thought to myself. The mayor is going to stay for the rest of the welcoming activities before taking off.

Much to my surprise, the mayor not only stayed the whole first day of the conference, but was visibly present the next morning as well. I was intrigued enough to seek him out during the first break of that second day. "Your Honor," I said after introducing myself as a first time conference attendee, "I was really impressed that you were with us the whole day yesterday, but I have to say that I am blown away that you're back with us today." I received a warm smile and a look that made it appear he was perplexed by what I just said. "How's that?" he said.

"Well your Honor," I replied, "I'd be hard pressed to imagine most mayors staying for an entire day, let alone attending the entire conference." The Mayor furrowed his brow for a moment, staring at the ground. He then lifted his head and, with a twinkle in his eyes, asked me in reply, "Well, where on earth would it be more important for them to be?" In an instant I knew that at least half of Clemson's successful town-gown formula had been revealed to me. The principal leader of the community embraced the campus as a full partner. And according to my colleague and friend Jeff Martin (who currently serves as one of Clemson University's assistant vice presidents for advancement), the university's longstanding and reciprocal embrace of the Clemson community completes the equation of how this particular town-gown relationship has evolved into one of the premier examples of campuses and communities working and living in harmony with one another.

If there is a "secret recipe" for success, its main ingredient is leadership that cares about town-gown relationships. In order to present evidence about the degree to which leadership matters in this regard, this next section of the book is an extension of previously published work in the journal *Innovative Higher Education* that I co-authored with Dr. Mike Fox and Dr. Jeff Martin in early 2014.

In that original article, we laid out case examples of the four different town-gown types using our three home institutions plus an additional fourth university (Queens) that Dr. Fox knew quite well. Our intention was to provide brief illustrations of what each theoretical town-gown type looked like in actual practice. That said, we stated emphatically that these were "snapshots" of where a given campus-community relationship existed at a single moment in time (in this case, the 2012-2013 academic year in which this paper was written). We were careful in stating this caveat because we are well aware of the impact that changes in effort and comfort levels can and will do to alter town-gown relationships, and thus the typologies they represent, over time.

Clemson University and the city of Clemson, South Carolina (USA) served as our example of the harmonious town-gown relationship, characterized by higher levels of effort and higher levels of comfort. Our example of a traditional town-gown relationship was Mount Allison University and the town of Sackville, New Brunswick (Canada), marked by lower levels of effort and moderately high levels of comfort. Queens University, located in Kingston, Ontario (Canada), became our example of the conflicted town-gown relationship, characterized by higher levels of effort and lower levels of comfort. Finally, The Ohio State University at Mansfield regional campus, located in Mansfield, Ohio (USA) served as our example of the devitalized town-gown relationship, marked by lower levels of effort and lower levels of comfort.

The original writing that Dr. Fox and Dr. Martin did on their home institutions had to be rather radically reduced in order to fit the page restrictions of the journal in which our co-authored article was published. To expand upon our original writing, these colleagues agreed to allow me to use an extended amount of this material in this book in order to elaborate the connection between leadership and the quality of town-gown relationships as illustrated by the traditional and conflicted types. In each of these first two case examples, the emphasis was on culling additional historical information; that is, I selected material that served to illustrate the kinds of interactions that campus and community leaders experienced with one another that created the context for the town-gown relationship type described in the Gavazzi, Fox, and Martin paper.

The third case example regarding the conflicted town-gown relationship was written by Dr. Fox due to his familiarity with the association between Queens University and the city of Kingston, Ontario. Because Dr. Fox's writing on this particular campus-community interaction was both succinct and specifically focused on leadership issues, a substantial portion of the Gavazzi, Fox, and Martin article dealing with this town-gown relationship is re-introduced in a manner that is quite similar to the way it was originally presented in the journal.

Last but not least, I attempted to expand upon my own original writing as the local expert on the case example related to the devitalized relationship type I had inherited in 2011 as I assumed the responsibilities of Dean and Director of the Ohio State Mansfield campus. By any stretch of the imagination, the description of what I found upon my arrival is not a complimentary one. Happily, however, the update of this situation (provided in chapter 8) exemplifies the fact that town-gown relationships can and do change over time... especially with a lot of work!

Harmonious Relationship Example: Clemson University and the City of Clemson, South Carolina, United States of America

"The City of Clemson (population 14,000) and Clemson University (17,000 undergraduate students) is perhaps the ideal example for discussing what a harmonious town-gown relationship looks like... both entities were fortunate to have farsighted leaders who set the framework for good communication and actions. The dedication and high degree of effort to pursue common solutions to the challenges continued to develop over the years, resulting in an ever increasing level of comfort between the partners as they worked together. In essence, this search for

shared goals and objectives was the initial phase in the development of what has

become an outstanding example of a harmonious town-gown relationship."

(Gavazzi, Fox, & Martin, 2014, p. 371).

What kinds of interactions have campus and community leaders experienced with one another that created the context for the harmonious type described in the Gavazzi, Fox, and Martin paper?

Jeff Martin's original description of the city of Clemson and Clemson University included a great deal of emphasis on how various leadership structures were intertwined in both formal and informal ways. On the more formal side, the city manager and the president of the local chamber of commerce sit as official members of the university president's cabinet, and historically have been encouraged to be actively involved in any and all decision-making processes that concern town-gown issues. Less formally, but by no means less significantly, faculty and staff employees of Clemson University often as not serve as elected officials on the Clemson city council.

As a result, campus and community representatives routinely talk about business being conducted by "the Clemson Family," a viewpoint that has given rise to a number of shared city and university traditions for solving problems and making decisions in the town-gown realm. In turn, this framework for power sharing between the campus and the community has empowered leadership at the presidential and mayoral levels to regularly seek each other's opinions and advice.

In 1985, this cooperative context became institutionalized through the establishment of the Joint City/University Advisory Board (JCUAB). The JCUAB was comprised of equal numbers of city and university employees, and was headed by leaders from the city council, the community police force, and the university president's council. At first, the JCUAB mission was to serve as a "problem solving advisory" group on town-gown issues. The charter statement contained specific language that included fostering positive town-gown communication, improving resource utilization, identifying opportunities that would mutually benefit both the campus and community, and suggesting approaches to shared problems and concerns.

Five years later, however, the JCUAB scope evolved. The mission was expanded to go beyond advisory capacity and become the official body of leaders who would study town-gown issues and make recommendations for action to be taken by the city council and president's cabinet. The scope of responsibility for the JCUAB group was outlined in a memorandum of understanding that was signed by both the mayor and the university president. This MOU contained a clear articulation of issues that are instantly recognizable by anyone familiar with town-gown issues: land use, student housing, transportation and parking, security and public safety, and public works and utilities.

A few years later, the JCUAB mission expanded again as the group was tasked with the study of potential new partnership opportunities for the city and university. One item taken up almost immediately by this group involved the possibility of creating a combined transportation system, which eventually led to the city-managed Clemson Area Transit (CAT) system that serves both the campus and community. Shared services issues also were taken up by the JCUAB members, leading to the consolidation of fire protection services under university management that serves both the campus and community.

In sum, we see that the campus and community leaders were that engaged in activities with one another that reflected both high effort and high comfort levels. In this case, the harmonious town-gown relationship was built largely on the development of a joint planning group that tackled issues of importance to both the university and the community. Further, the evolving nature of that planning group's mission and scope would seem to reflect the growing trust and confidence that town and gown partners must experience with one another for a harmonious relationship to emerge and become solidified over time.

Traditional Relationship Example: Mount Allison University and the City of Sackville, New Brunswick, Canada

"Founded in 1839, Mount Allison University sits on the high ground in the center of Sackville, New Brunswick, Canada (population 5,000); and it actually predates the town, which was incorporated in 1903… The most notable aspect of this traditional town and gown relationship is its stability, especially that of the various actors and processes within the community. The Mayor of the Town had previously worked for over forty years in the University facilities management department… In turn, the University president is finishing his second five-year term and represents an on-going line of presidents who have presided over steady budgets, sizable endowments, no debt, and the prized top spot in the national university rankings. Amidst these calm waters, however, the Mayor and the President and their administrations have not met formally in years and have given almost no attention of note to shared governance or community-based activities." (Gavazzi, Fox, & Martin, 2014, p. 370).

What kinds of interactions have campus and community leaders experienced with one another that created the context for the traditional type described in the Gavazzi, Fox, and Martin paper?

The original description of this traditional town and gown relationship offered by Mike Fox emphasized the stability of leadership on both sides of the town-gown equation. For example, the mayor of Sackville at the time the *Innovative Higher Education* article was written had first worked as a university facilities management department for his entire career. Further, this mayor was born and raised in Sackville, and before being elected mayor had served more than a decade on town council.

Likewise, the university president was finishing his second five-year term at the time the *Innovative Higher Education* article originally was drafted. Both he and his predecessors represent an on-going line of presidents who have chosen to remain at the university for rather elongated periods of time, bucking a trend that has witnessed university presidents across North America staying in office for ever shorter periods of time.

The town-gown relationship as a whole has been described not only as stable, but also as congenial. There are numerous events and student-focused activities that are put on and attended by both campus and community representatives. For instance, the Sackville town council and various service groups in town have hosted a corn boil as a welcoming event for new Mount Allison students. In turn, the campus puts on concerts and hosts sporting events that are attended as much by local residents as they are by students and faculty members.

At the same time, however, there is a disconnectedness within the town-gown relationship. There is a strong sense that events such as the ones described in the previous paragraph happen either "on campus" or "off campus" (and never the twain shall meet, as one local wag put it). This is traced back to the fact that there is no shared governance structure to deal with town-gown issues that arise, nor is there any sort of joint planning committee that would serve to coordinate campus and community events and activities.

Most pointedly, the mayor and the president have not met formally in years, and previous campus and community leaders have described the relationship between town and gown as "two solitudes" at best. The term "benign neglect" also has been offered as a less flattering way to describe the town-gown relationship. In essence, each leader has pursued their own agendas and objectives without consulting the other party.

More recently, however, the mayor and council members did in fact reach out to the university at the same time that they were launching a strategic planning process for the town of Sackville. In turn, they were able to recruit specific representatives from university administration and student government, as well as a more general pool of faculty and staff members, onto the planning committee.

In part as a result, a five-point strategic plan was developed that included one objective aimed at "strengthening the existing working relationship between Mount Allison University and the Town of Sackville." More specifically, this particular objective included language that sought to develop a shared mission for the town's distinct identity as a destination to live, work, and study. It also emphasized the desire to create better town-gown partnerships and take advantage of shared service opportunities between the town and the university wherever possible.

A series of unfortunate events unraveled this promising endeavor, however. First and foremost, a newly elected town council largely ignored the strategic plan developed by their predecessors. Second, unbeknownst to anyone in the community at the time, the university had launched its own strategic planning process. The university's outreach and engagement with the community was so minimal, and the dearth of thought given to the town-gown relationship so profound, that the final campus document failed to even state that Mount Allison University was located in the town of Sackville.

In sum, we find here a town-gown relationship characterized by relatively low levels of shared activities in combination with modest comfort levels. Recent attempts by university and municipal leaders to more fully engage each other seemed to have withered over time. As a result, the campus and community continues to remain somewhat amicably disengaged with one another in a traditional town-gown relationship.

Conflicted Relationship Example: Queens University and the City of Kingston, Ontario, Canada

"Without a doubt, the most infamous conflicted town and gown relationship in

Canada involves the City of Kingston, Ontario (population 123,000) and Queen's

University (full-time student population of 21,000). Founded in 1841, the

University has been engaged in what has been described as a "history of conflict"

(Stechyson, 2010) throughout much of its existence in contemporary times."

(Gavazzi, Fox, & Martin, 2014, p. 369).

What kinds of interactions have campus and community leaders experienced with one another that created the context for the conflicted type described in the Gavazzi, Fox, and Martin paper?

If the misbehaviors of your students are reported regularly in newspaper headlines, it's likely as not that your campus and community presently are involved in a conflicted relationship. For Queens University and the city of Kingston, Ontario, the events on and near campus during each fall orientation and homecoming celebration received significant negative media attention over the years. Excessive drinking, extreme noise, broken glass, and burning automobiles had been the backdrop of each story, with hundreds of students being arrested by riot police as the main act. This despite millions of dollars having been spent on potential solutions to these destructive activities.

According to Mike Fox's original write-up of this situation in the 2014

Innovative Higher Education article, one of the corresponding difficulties experienced by this campus and community has been the regular turnover in leadership positions. Some of the more recent principals (the university's term for their president) have been relative short-timers, for instance, in addition to the regular turnover resulting from electoral changes in municipal government. Partly as a result, there had been little contact (let alone coordination of activities) between the town and gown leaders.

Nature abhors a vacuum and, as a result, a number of neighborhood associations became very active in using various media outlets to complain about student misbehavior. Among other things, these groups began to pressure community leaders and the police to adopt much more aggressive and punitive methods to deal with students. In reaction, homecoming and related activities were suspended by the campus for a number of years. This at the very least would have seemed to represent a positive move by the university to not only acknowledge the fact that the university was creating a large problem, but also to take some initial steps to preempt the difficulties surrounding those autumn events.

In 2007, campus and community leaders began to discuss a more coordinated approach to a variety of town-gown issues. Led by the University Principal, Vice-Principal, Mayor, and the Chief Administrative Officer of Kingston, a committee was formed in order to study the issues and make recommendations that would move the town-gown relationship toward more solid footing with one another. Working over the course of three years with various stakeholder groups that included students and neighborhood associations, these efforts resulted in the *2011-2014 City of Kingston Town and Gown Strategic Plan.*

Rolled out with great fanfare, the new strategic town and gown plan seemed to create a sense of goodwill and hope for a better and brighter future. A new University Principal recently had been hired, and he gave assurances that he would work closely within the guidelines of the new plan in order to better connect the campus with the community. In turn, the town elected a new mayor who was a Queen's alumnus, generating significant optimism that a new day was dawning in the relationship between the university and Kingston.

Not long afterwards, however, things began to fall apart in short order. The Principal unilaterally reinstated the homecoming activities in the fall of 2013 without consulting city leaders or preparing local residents. As was stated in our 2014 *Innovative Higher Education* article:

> *"At a subsequent event in early October of 2013, thousands of students and alumni returned to the neighborhoods surrounding the university. The Mayor went to the heart of the student ghetto late on one particular Saturday night and sent out a tweet directed at the University Principal that stated; "I have two words*

for you: NOT GOOD," it said. The hardline positions of town against gown had, once again, been drawn" (p. 370).

In sum, we find a town-gown relationship with a long history of issues and concerns that have generated low comfort levels in the midst of high levels of conflict. The steps undertaken by both university and municipal leaders to soften well-known friction points were well-intended, to be sure. Regrettably, however, those efforts could not be sustained, and the campus and community partners found themselves once again fighting old battles.

Devitalized Relationship Example: The Ohio State University at Mansfield and the City of Mansfield, Ohio, United States of America

"Founded in 1959, The Ohio State University at Mansfield by design provides affordable access to the state's flagship research university for approximately 1,500 students who either are location bound or need an alternative regional campus entry point when the selective admissions process to the flagship campus does not tilt in their favor. Mansfield, Ohio is the county seat and former manufacturing giant (top 10 in the United States during the 1950's) with 47,000 current residents… there is a history of psychological disappointments that have contributed to discomfort and an increasingly devitalized relationship between campus and community over time, despite the initial energy expended on making the relationship work." (Gavazzi, Fox, & Martin, 2014, p. 367).

Question: What kinds of interactions have campus and community leaders experienced with one another that created the context for the devitalized type described in the Gavazzi, Fox, and Martin paper?

In this case study of the association between the Ohio State Mansfield campus and its surrounding communities, we witness the experience of loss and disappointment as the main driver of the devitalized relationship that ensued. In large part, this disenchanted relationship was predicated on several interrelated issues surrounding a local hospital and its nursing program, which for many years had relied on the Ohio State Mansfield campus to provide the general education courses for its students.

In late 2008, administrators from the hospital and nursing program had reached out to Ohio State in order to explore the possibility of becoming more firmly connected programmatically. A plan had been drawn up that would include the hospital constructing a new building on the Ohio State Mansfield campus, maintaining programmatic oversight but opening its doors to increased numbers of students from Ohio State and North Central State College (the co-located technical college) wishing to become nurses. By all accounts given by those higher education officials involved in the negotiations at that time, the original plan was an exciting three-way partnership opportunity.

Unfortunately, these same sources went on to report that the hospital leadership team unexpectedly made a unilateral decision to withdraw from the collaborative deal that had been struck. Instead, the hospital board members proposed that The Ohio State University take over the program altogether and fold it into its existing College of Nursing (run on the Columbus campus). No one at Ohio State saw this one coming. In fact, the plan to build and maintain a partnership under the original terms already had been carefully vetted and approved at all levels of the university's administration. In essence, everyone within the Ohio State system thought this was a done deal.

In response to the revised proposal offered by the hospital's board, university officials on the Columbus campus raised significant concerns about how the students and faculty involved in the hospital's nursing program would be folded into the structure of Ohio State. This was not going to be a hindrance to the partnership as long as the hospital maintained oversight of the nursing school, including the management of its accreditation process. With the proposed change in ownership of the nursing program, however, the tables had been turned. The hospital leaders wanted Ohio State to take over the day-to-day operation of the program.

The end of this particular part of the story is not a pretty one. The Dean of Ohio State's College of Nursing declined to consider such a proposal, and despite a series of meetings held with various university leaders, no champion for this cause emerged on the Columbus campus.

Regrettably, the official answer to the hospital's new offer from Ohio State administrators by midyear 2009 was of the "thanks but no thanks" variety. In response, a local private university was officially approached with a similar request to take over the nursing program. An agreement was quickly formalized between the hospital and the private university administration by early 2010. That private university immediately launched an aggressive capital campaign to raise funds for the new building, which was to be constructed on land that the hospital owned approximately 4 miles from the Ohio State Mansfield campus.

This was a public relations nightmare for the Ohio State leadership. Despite the fact that the hospital board unilaterally changed the nature of the deal to be struck, all of the blame was placed on Ohio State for failing to take over the nursing program. In addition to the general ill will expressed toward Ohio State by many residents at the time, there also were some immediately recognizable consequences that arose as backlash from the community. Most pointedly, a civic group – comprised of many local business leaders who served as some of the largest philanthropists in the greater Mansfield geographic area – accelerated the private university's request to be the focus of the community's primary giving efforts in order to provide assistance for the construction project that would build the new nursing school building. As if to underscore the point being made about where blame was being placed, many of Ohio State's biggest local supporters agreed to join the private university's capital campaign as volunteers and benefactors.

As the dust settled, the campus and community adopted a pattern of interaction that reflected low levels of both effort and comfort, the classic portrait of the devitalized town-gown relationship. While this was the situation I inherited at the beginning of 2011 when I took over as the senior administrator of the Ohio State Mansfield campus, it was by no means the end of the story. The happier tale of redemption and reengagement of the campus and community partners can be found at the beginning of chapter eight.

Summary

The main objective of this chapter was to put forward a new way of understanding town-gown relationships through use of the marriage metaphor. Two critical dimensions (effort and comfort levels) were used in combination to illustrate four types of town-gown relationships: harmonious, traditional, conflicted, and devitalized. Theoretical descriptions of these four town-gown types were followed by actual case examples. Special attention was given to the critical role that university and municipal leaders play in terms of determining the quality of campus-community

interactions over time.

5. MEASURING TOWN-GOWN RELATIONSHIPS

The main objective of this book's fifth chapter is to take away the guesswork that typically accompanies attempts to describe and define town-gown relationships by inviting readers to become more data-driven in their approach. The development of the Optimal College Town Assessment (OCTA) grew out of the need to operationalize and quantify variation in campus and community member perceptions of town-gown characteristics. In addition to adopting the Gavazzi, Fox, and Martin (2014) conceptualization of campus-community relationships as the combination of effort and comfort levels (as described in chapter four), this measurement effort was designed to capture participants' direct personal experiences of these two dimensions, as well as their opinions about overall community sensitivities. Further, construction of the OCTA was intended to provide some discrimination among and between the different groups that comprise the campus and community stakeholders whose perspectives are solicited in this sort of data-gathering process.

The 16 Core OCTA Questions

The measurement of perceptions of effort and comfort levels regarding relationships between community members and each of four campus representative types (students, faculty, leaders/administrative staff, and governing board members) included the following four primary questions:

- How much personal contact do you have with each group of campus representatives (assessed on a five-point Likert-type scale ranging from "no contact" to "a great deal of contact")?
- How active do you believe each group of campus representatives is in terms of contributing to the well-being of the community as a whole (assessed on a five-point Likert-type scale ranging from "not active" to "very active")?
- How would you rate your own personal relationships with each group of campus representatives (assessed on a five-point Likert-type scale ranging from "very negative" to "neutral" to "very positive")?
- How would you rate the relationships between each group of campus representatives and the community as a whole (assessed on a five-point Likert-type scale ranging from "very negative" to "neutral" to "very positive")?

For *community residents*, the 16 core OCTA questions include the following:

How much **personal contact** do you have with the following groups of people from campus?

No contact		Moderate		A great deal of contact
0	1	2	3	4

1. Students from the campus?

0	1	2	3	4

2. Faculty from the campus?

0	1	2	3	4

3. Administrators/staff members from the campus?

0	1	2	3	4

4. Governing board members of the campus?

0	1	2	3	4

How active do you believe the following groups of people from campus are in terms of **contributing to the well-being** of the **community as a whole?**

Not active		Moderately active		Very active
0	1	2	3	4

5. Students from the campus?

0	1	2	3	4

6. Faculty from the campus?

0	1	2	3	4

7. Administrators/staff members from the campus?

0	1	2	3	4

8. Governing board members of the campus?

0	1	2	3	4

On a scale ranging from very negative to very positive, how would you rate your **own personal relationships** with the following groups of people from campus?

Very negative	Slightly negative	Neutral	Slightly positive	Very positive
1	2	3	4	5

9. Students from the campus?

1	2	3	4	5

10. Faculty from the campus?

1	2	3	4	5

11. Administrators/staff members from the campus?

1	2	3	4	5

12. Governing board members of the campus?

1	2	3	4	5

On a scale ranging from very negative to very positive, how would you rate the relationships between the following groups of people from campus and the **community as a whole?**

Very negative	Slightly negative	Neutral	Slightly positive	Very positive
1	2	3	4	5

13. Students from the campus?

1	2	3	4	5

14. Faculty from the campus?

1	2	3	4	5

15. Administrators/staff members from the campus?

1	2	3	4	5

16. Governing board members of the campus?

1	2	3	4	5

For *campus representatives*, the 16 core OCTA questions include the following:

How much **personal contact** do you have with the following groups of people in the community?

No contact		Moderate		A great deal of contact
0	1	2	3	4

1. Business and industry leaders?

0	1	2	3	4

2. Elected government officials?

0	1	2	3	4

3. Teachers and administrators of local school districts?

0	1	2	3	4

4. Members of civic organizations and non-profits serving the community?

0	1	2	3	4

How much **overall contact** do you believe **the campus** has with the following groups of people in the community?

No contact		Moderate		A great deal of contact
0	1	2	3	4

5. Business and industry leaders?

0	1	2	3	4

6. Elected government officials?

0	1	2	3	4

7. Teachers and administrators of local school districts?

0	1	2	3	4

8. Members of civic organizations and non-profits serving the community?

0	1	2	3	4

On a scale ranging from very negative to very positive, how would you rate your **own personal relationships** with the following groups of people in the community?

Very negative	Slightly negative	Neutral	Slightly positive	Very positive
1	2	3	4	5

9. Business and industry leaders?

1	2	3	4	5

10. Elected government officials?

1	2	3	4	5

11. Teachers and administrators of local school districts?

1	2	3	4	5

12. Members of civic organizations and non-profits serving the community?

1	2	3	4	5

On a scale ranging from very negative to very positive, how would you rate the relationships between **the campus as a whole** and the following groups of people in the community?

Very negative	Slightly negative	Neutral	Slightly positive	Very positive
1	2	3	4	5

13. Business and industry leaders?

1	2	3	4	5

14. Elected government officials?

1	2	3	4	5

15. Teachers and administrators of local school districts?

1	2	3	4	5

16. Members of civic organizations and non-profits serving the community?

1	2	3	4	5

Initial Findings

The Ohio State Mansfield regional campus was used as the focal point of the first pilot study using the OCTA items, as well as residents of the three communities surrounding the campus (the more scientifically based report on this study can be found in the 2015 Gavazzi and Fox article published in the journal *Innovative Higher Education*). The campus exists within the geographical boundaries of the City of Mansfield (50,000 citizens). The City of Ontario (6,000 citizens) is situated just beyond campus property on the Northwest side, and the City of Shelby (9,000 citizens) is located approximately 6 miles away. Taken together, these three municipalities have come to be considered as part of the "Campus District."

The campus administrative leadership approached a variety of local organizations in order to solicit participation in the OCTA designed to examine the ways that campus and community relationships are perceived by community members from the three cities making up the Campus District. Particular attention was paid to the Chamber of Commerce, school districts, and the local United Way in the hopes of attracting significant participation by business owners, educators, and leaders of non-profit agencies. These three groups were deemed to be particularly important stakeholders to take the survey because they were most likely to have contact with students from the campus. Among other things, this thinking was based on the knowledge of the rather significant numbers of students taking part in such activities as the business and industry internship initiative, student teaching placements that were part of our teacher preparation program, and a mandatory community service experience that social science majors and social work majors were required to obtain prior to graduation.

The participants in the survey included 602 individuals employed within one of the three cities making up the Campus District who agreed to take part in the study (a total of 775 citizens initially had responded to the survey, but only those cases with complete data sets were kept for further analysis purposes). Participants chose to visit the survey's website as a response to email invitations and media advertisements regarding the survey effort. The study included 433 (72%) individuals employed in Mansfield, 60 (10%) individuals employed in Ontario, and 109 (18%) individuals employed in Shelby. The sample included 209 teachers and school administrators (35%), 56 leaders of non-profit organizations (9%), and 50 business owners (8%) in addition to the 287 individuals (48%) claiming none of these particular professional roles in the campus district.

Variables in the Pilot Study

An index containing participant responses to each of the four primary questions described at the beginning of this chapter was created by summing the four items pertaining to each of the campus representative types inside of each primary question, yielding a score for personal contact, community contact, personal comfort, and community comfort. Next, the personal and community scores regarding the effort and comfort dimensions were combined to create an overall index of total effort and total comfort levels.

Personal and Community Effort and Comfort Levels

Personal contact and personal comfort with campus representatives were significantly and positively associated with one another, an indication that greater contact between campus and community members is related to increased relationship satisfaction. A similar association was detected between the community effort and community comfort variables. The more modest correlations generated between the personal effort and community effort variables and the personal comfort and the community comfort variables provided some initial evidence that participants were able to discriminate between their personal dealings with various campus representatives and what they believed the overall community experienced inside of these town-gown relationships.

A breakdown of the personal effort and community effort variables indicated some interesting variation by campus representative type. Effort as personal contact with students was rated at the highest levels, followed by faculty members, administrative leaders and staff, and board members. In turn, administrators and staff were perceived as having made most of the efforts that contributed to the well-being of the community as a whole, followed closely by the efforts of students, faculty members, and then board members. The general pattern of results for the personal comfort and community comfort variables indicated that personal and community comfort levels are highest with students, followed by faculty members, administrative leaders and staff, and board members.

Finally, the theoretical range of the total effort and total comfort variables is 0 to 32. The mean score of the total effort variable (8.95) fell under the mid-point (16) on the effort dimension, while the mean score of the total comfort variable (20.05) fell above the mid-point (16) of the comfort dimension. The resulting combination of lower effort and higher comfort level scores indicated that the campus and community were involved in a *traditional* town-gown relationship type at the time of the survey.

Variation as a Function of Distance and Role

It was thought that perceptions of effort and comfort levels would vary as a function of geographic location. More specifically, it was believed that individuals located in the closest municipality to the campus – in this

88

case Mansfield – would report higher levels of both effort and comfort in comparison to individuals located in Ontario and Shelby. Results indicated significant differences on the total effort variable as a function of location. As predicted, perceived effort levels were highest in Mansfield, followed by Ontario, and then Shelby, the exact order of distance from campus. In addition, total comfort levels also followed the exact order of distance from the campus.

Some additional exploratory analyses were conducted using a sub-sample containing only those individuals who had identified themselves as educators, leaders of non-profit organizations, and business owners. Results of further testing found significant differences on the total comfort variable as a function of role. Perceived comfort levels were highest among business owners, followed by non-profit leaders, and then educators. Further comparisons of the three groups indicated that the educators reported significantly lower effort levels than did both the non-profit leaders and the business leaders.

Additional Analyses

The original 16 OCTA questions employed in the first pilot study described above were augmented with some qualitative questions that were designed to give respondents greater latitude in describing campus-community relationships. This qualitative dataset and subsequent analyses were first reported by Gavazzi (2015a) in a paper for the journal *Planning for Higher Education* (published by the Society for College and University Planners). A total of 236 participants (39% of the original sample used in the first OCTA pilot study) also had responded in some fashion to an open-ended question (accompanied by an unlimited text box) at the end of the survey that asked: "Do you have any thoughts about what the campus might do in the future to improve relationships with the community?"

Content analysis procedures were employed to identify and organize themes that emerged from the transcribed text of all participant responses to this open-ended question. The following eight themes emerged from the final categories established through this process, followed by the number of responses and percentage of the total responses reflected by each category:

1. Engage in volunteer activities that increase visibility in the community

   (n = 71 or 30% of the sample)

2. Live in the community and spend money there

   (n = 41 or 17% of the sample)

3. Hold more events on campus

   (n = 36 or 15% of the sample)

4. Expand the number of classes and degrees offered on the campus

   (n = 25 or 11% of the sample)

5. Connect more with local school districts

    (n = 24 or 9% of the sample)

6. Generate more publicity about campus news and events

    (n = 20 or 8% of the sample)

7. Make coursework more affordable and accessible

    (n = 14 or 7% of the sample)

8. Offer faculty and staff expertise as applied to community needs

    (n = 5 or 2% of the sample)

All eight of the emergent themes are thought to be reflective of action items that, if implemented, could make a further contribution to perceptions of greater effort by campus representatives to connect with the community. In turn, the effective performance of these activities would generate even greater comfort levels as reported by stakeholders. Hence, we see here how the collection and analysis of qualitative data can directly enhance the use of the more quantitatively oriented OCTA.

The themes that emerged from these analyses generate a clearly defined set of plans for enhancing town-gown relationships. Interestingly, the most well subscribed theme that emerged – engaging in more volunteer activities that increase visibility – also would seem to be one of the least expensive to institute, at least in terms of financial costs. Here is an example of a response from this category:

"Give the community more reasons to feel like the campus is really a part of the community. Become more visible at community events, maybe even volunteer or help sponsor an event every once in a while."

Of course, volunteerism in any form is an expense of sorts (i.e. time is money), which is why it often is described as an *investment* in the well-being of the community. The offering of unpaid assistance to the community is embedded to a certain extent in other themes that emerged from the data. This includes both the theme concerning the need to connect to local school districts and the theme about offering of faculty and staff expertise as applied to community needs. Here are two examples from each of those latter categories respectively:

"Become resources in the classroom as mentors for the students; pair them with young and/or struggling readers and writers; help with math, etc."

"Becoming a solution to many of the community's problems makes (the campus) an invaluable tool for improving our community. Issues such as education, race, arts, social work etc. are wide open areas for (the campus) to make meaningful contributions to the community."

A more direct form of investment is found in the second most well subscribed category – living in the community and spending money there – where we see the emergence of a much more economically-based theme.

Beyond the very straightforward suggestions about residing within the immediate community surrounding the campus and buying locally, there were plenty of higher level responses having to do with workforce development such as this one:

"Listen to the community, especially the business community. Prepare students with real skills and learning experiences that will fit into the employer needs of 2014 and beyond. Encourage business and community leaders to understand ways to keep our best and brightest students in this community."

There is little surprise in finding responses that fit into categories representing higher education access and affordability – expanding the number of classes and degrees offered on campus and making them more affordable – as these are salient issues across the country right now. The examples of responses shared here from each of these categories respectively go beyond the simple treatise to "do more with less" in reflecting the desire to create higher aspirations for both individuals and the community as a whole:

"Create more opportunities for local degree completion relevant to community needs. Keep building up internships and other work experiences."

"I think that some residents still see higher education as unreachable. I think we need to make it reachable and demystify the process of moving into college."

The last two themes – holding more events on campus and generating more publicity about campus news and events – would seem to go hand in hand. The two comments from each of these categories included here reveal a desire on the part of community residents to feel welcome when they visit, and invited to do so.

"Create reasons for the community to come to the campus. Your location makes it hard to connect by accident - the interaction needs to be intentional."

"I'm not very aware of activities to connect the community to the campus, but I think they are happening. Perhaps more publicity would help. I think it is a matter of getting information out to the community and educating them on campus activities, opportunities and community events."

Summary

The main objective of this chapter was to help readers take the guesswork out of understanding the quality of town-gown relationships. In large part, this effort focused attention on the development of a standardized measurement tool known as the Optimal College Town Assessment, or OCTA. The original 16 items of the OCTA were supplied for use in two versions: one for campus representatives, and another for community members. The quantitative results of an initial pilot study using the OCTA items were reported in this chapter, including interesting variations in effort and comfort levels as a function of geographical distance

and participant role. More qualitative results also were presented, including

themes that were developed from community member perspectives on

what campus representatives could do to improve town-gown relationships.

6. THE TOWN-GOWN MOBILIZATION CYCLE

The main objective of this chapter is to underscore the importance of seeing data gathering as part of a larger process – a mobilization cycle – that involves partnerships between campus and community stakeholders. In an important way, these sorts of activities become a vivid reflection of the present state of the town-gown relationship itself. If you suspect that your campus and community are not currently operating within an optimal relationship environment at present, then the mobilization cycle likely will be harder to implement. The good news here is that this kind of up front hard work not only will generate important baseline data once you have completed the cycle, but also will lay the foundation for a much more optimal relationship to develop as a result. In other words, this is the kind of hard work that will really pay off in the long run.

The Town-Gown Relationship Mobilization Cycle

As noted in the previous chapter, the use of an assessment tool such as the OCTA takes the guesswork out of understanding the quality of the town-gown relationship by providing a standardized way of examining effort and comfort levels between and among various campus and community stakeholders. This sort of assessment activity serves as a baseline data-gathering strategy that can be repeated over time in order to mark progress in the development and maintenance of more positive and productive collaborations among higher education and municipal representatives.

Figure 3: The Town-Gown Mobilization Cycle

There are thought to be a number of important activities that can take place both *prior to* and *following* such assessment efforts that can augment the understanding and enhancement of town-gown relationships. While these activities are interconnected, there is a logical sequencing that can provide valuable assistance in planning for and implementing an overall engagement strategy for campus and community partners. As originally presented in the journal *Metropolitan Universities* (Gavazzi, 2015b), these activities are organized into a Town-Gown Relationship Mobilization Cycle as seen in Figure 3.

Awareness Raising

The first step of the Mobilization Cycle involves awareness-raising about the importance of enhancing the quality of relationships between the campus and community partners, and raises basic questions such as where (and how) we begin this kind of work. Here, the Mobilization Cycle is activated by increasing knowledge of and appreciation for the importance of focusing on the town-gown relationship itself. Of course, campus and community representatives will be all over the map in terms of readiness to focus on their relationships with one another. The common denominator, however, will be the recognition that the campus and community stand to gain much more by acting together than by standing apart.

There may need to be a "therapeutic" component to this type of work, especially for those campuses and communities with conflicted and devitalized relationship histories. Here, past disagreements and disappointments may need to be acknowledged by one or both parties before meaningful partnerships can be formulated. One particularly fitting framework for this sort of community conversation is that of Howard Zehr (2002), whose work on restorative justice principles introduces a process of "healing the harm" that allows various parties to move beyond past grievances and toward more constructive engagement.

Coalition Building

The second step of the Mobilization Cycle involves coalition building, with particular attention paid to the identification of the primary campus and community stakeholders who will participate in various relationship-building activities, including the engagement of potential participants in surveying activities. This phase of the Mobilization Cycle involves a determination of who will be targeted in local data gathering efforts, which should be strongly related to the partners that will be approached in order to get the kind of campus and community participation that is necessary to create a meaningful (and hopefully representative) sample of stakeholders. In parallel fashion, this step also should involve the recognition of intended audiences who will be asked to listen to (and hopefully respond to) information generated throughout the data-gathering process.

Data Gathering

Data gathering represents the "middle ground" of the Mobilization Cycle. As the third step, it is preceded by activities designed to maximize access to key representatives on the campus and in the community. The ultimate success of this entire effort, in fact, rests on obtaining high quality data from the respondents themselves. Much of the work on the OCTA to date has been aimed at establishing a standardized baseline of the quality of campus-community partnerships. The OCTA items are available for use by individuals who are interested in the assessment of town-gown relationships, and over time will allow users to compare and contrast findings across settings and institutions. As noted in chapter four, however, this quantitative approach can and should be balanced by the collection of more qualitatively oriented information. This latter effort would be especially important in terms of developing a better understanding of the idiosyncratic needs and wishes of campuses and communities as they seek to better interact with one another.

Interpretation of Data

The fourth step of the Mobilization Cycle is centered on the interpretation of information that has been collected about campus and community perceptions of the town-gown relationships. Here, the quantitative and qualitative data must be organized, analyzed and reported on in some manner that is both understandable and immediately applicable to the intended audience of campus and community stakeholders. This phase of the Mobilization Cycle should involve the creation of relatively straightforward and easy to understand reports on sample demographics, methods, and results of interest to varied audiences. In addition, wherever possible graphs and other visual aids should be employed alongside text descriptions of the information. Pictures are indeed worth a thousand words, especially for community stakeholders who typically are unfamiliar with research and evaluation jargon.

Creating an Action Plan

The fifth and final step involves an evidence-based call to action, answering the fundamental question: "Now what?" This last phase of the Mobilization Cycle focuses attention on the development of next steps in the process of engaging campus and community partners. One of the keys to success here is remaining data-driven: being led by facts (i.e., the survey results) instead of feelings (i.e. someone's hunches, gut feelings, or recollections). On a related note, if the survey results end up raising as many questions as it answers, some further data-gathering may be in order. For example, perhaps a key constituent group was overlooked, resulting in the need for more quantitative data to be gathered from additional respondents. Alternatively, even greater attention might be paid to the collection of more elaborate qualitative information that would help to flesh out the initial quantitative findings. In this latter case, the use of focus groups would be an especially effective means by which to gain a richer understanding of town-gown relationship characteristics and pressing issues.

Applying the Mobilization Cycle: A Case Study

The Ohio State Mansfield regional campus and its co-located technical college – North Central State College – are the focus of our case study example regarding the application of the mobilization cycle. This information originally was presented in the journal *Access*, a newer research periodical published by the National Association of Branch Campus Administrators. At the time this description was written (Gavazzi, 2015c), the regional campus served approximately 1,200 students, about 75% of whom attended in a fulltime capacity. In turn, the technical college served around 3,000 mostly part-time students. A shared service agreement bound these two institutions together at the physical facilities level since the technical college came into existence in the mid-1970s. More recently, however, the development of a number of 2+2 programs in conjunction with a series of joint community development activities (one particularly popular example is a combined business and industry internship initiative mentioned previously in this book) have further strengthened the partnership between the two institutions.

Phase 1: Awareness-Raising

The fact that these particular two institutions of higher learning were making significant strides toward increased partnerships became one of the compelling reasons for conducting the community survey together. In essence, the members of each institution's senior leadership team were interested in gaining a better understanding of the degree to which community stakeholders perceived their relationships with the college and university in both similar and different ways. There was a history of disconnectedness (and at times outright hostility) between the two institutions under previous administrations, so there was some real concern regarding the residual effects of that time period. Therefore, it was thought that a lot would be gained by approaching the community as partners regarding the survey effort, while at the same time working to establish some baseline understanding of what the town-gown relationship looked like at present for each institution.

As well, there was great importance attached to understanding potential differences in perceptions of the town-gown relationship as a function of the distinct groups of community stakeholders who would be participating in the survey. Both institutions placed significant numbers of students in business and industry internships, in service learning courses that were situated within non-profit agencies, and in local school districts as a function of early child education and teacher preparation programs. Therefore, senior administrative leadership decided very early on to focus special attention on the relationships between the higher education institutions and these three particular groups of community stakeholders.

To get the word out on the survey specifically and the importance of paying attention to the relationships between campus representatives and community members more generally, the assistance of various print and electronic media partners was enlisted by senior leaders from both co-located institutions. This included straightforward public service announcements and advertisements, as well as making senior administrators available for interviews and otherwise supplying content for stories to be generated about both the survey and various town-gown activities that were ongoing.

Phase 2: Coalition Building

As the publicity efforts were set into motion, the senior administrators of both institutions began to meet directly with community leaders. Because there were three separate local governments within a 10 mile radius of the campus, meetings were set with the town managers and city council members of all three entities, as well as with the county commissioners. Face-to-face appointments also were made with the leaders of the three main groups of community stakeholders identified above:

business owners, non-profit leaders, and local school districts. For the sake of efficiency, the Chamber of Commerce and the local economic development group were the points of contact for the business community. Similarly, the local United Way became the touchstone for entry into the non-profit sector. And finally, individual appointments were scheduled with each of the local school district superintendents.

During these meetings, the senior higher education administrators began by reviewing what information was known about current contacts occurring between campus representatives and community members affiliated with each specific group. Next, help was requested from community leaders in the form of an agreement to use their email lists and various social media outlets to promote the participation of their affiliates in the community survey. Assurances then were given that the groups would have full access to the survey results, as well as the offer to conduct follow-up meetings with their constituents in order to address any and all issues and concerns brought out through the survey.

Phase 3: Data Gathering

A beta version of the web-based Optimal College Town Assessment (OCTA) was employed in the data collection phase of this initiative, the findings of which were introduced in the fourth chapter of this book. The data collection site was open for a two week period, and a total of 775 community members chose to participate in the survey within this time period. The sample contained 602 individuals who answered every item in the survey, including 50 business owners, 56 non-profit leaders, and 209 educators, as well as 287 community residents who did not self-report an affiliation with any of those three employment groups.

Phase 4: Data Interpretation

The mean scores for both the four year and two year institutions on the effort dimension represented moderately low levels. Additionally, the mean scores for both the four year and two year institutions on the comfort dimension represented moderately high levels. Taken together, the combination of lower effort and higher comfort placed both the college and university within the traditional town-gown relationship type.

As noted earlier, further examination of the effort and comfort scores among the three major stakeholder groups (business owners, non-profit leaders, local educators) was revealing. Business owners reported the highest amount of effort, followed by non-profit leaders, and then educators. This pattern of results was significant for both the two year and four year institutions, and further analyses revealed that the significant results were a function of the difference between the scores of the business owners and the educators. In essence, it seemed to be the case that the co-located partners were doing the best job relating to the business community in comparison to all other stakeholders at the time of the survey.

For the comfort dimension the same pattern of results was repeated for the two year institution. Business owners reported the highest amount of comfort, followed by non-profit leaders, and then educators. This pattern of results was significant and further analyses again revealed that the significant results were a function of the difference between the scores of the business owners and the educators. Interestingly, there were no significant differences among the three groups on the comfort dimension for the four year institution.

These and other results were shared in a variety of ways with campus and community stakeholders in the months following the survey. This included the dissemination of a written report, a town hall meeting (with PowerPoint slides that subsequently were shared via email), and a series of interviews granted to local media representatives that were turned into print and broadcast stories.

Phase 5: Evidence-Based Action Planning

The significantly higher effort and comfort scores reported by business owners became a rallying point regarding the planning for next steps in the process of enhancing town-gown relationships. In combination with the extremely popular business and industry internship program mentioned earlier, emerging partnerships between the campus and private developers of land holdings immediately adjacent to campus necessitated an intensification of activities with members of the business community and locally elected officials.

Collectively, these land use projects contributed to the creation of the Campus District. Precious little attention had been paid to the properties near the campus in previous years; that is, until the brand-new off-campus student housing complex described in chapter 2 was built. The housing initiative in and of itself was a substantial test of the resolve of the campus and community partners to work together. More specifically, there were a variety of infrastructure issues that had to be tackled, including most notably sewer connections that crossed municipal boundaries. Fortunately, the good will toward the campus as revealed in the community survey data was borne out. The utility issues were resolved fairly quickly, allowing the building construction to move forward.

The fact that upwards of 500 new residential students would soon be living in one concentrated area immediately adjacent to the campus entrance provided all the incentive that was needed for other development projects to be placed on the drawing board. To allay fears that retail projects would spring up in a haphazard manner, the campus lent its internal resources to a systematic planning process for the district. This included the adoption of the entire county by students in an upper level undergraduate city and regional planning course, an economic development plan drawn up by MBA students, and ongoing informal consultation given by professional planners from the university's main campus.

Out of these activities arose a Campus District Joint Planning Group, attended by government officials from the two municipalities within the geographic area defined by the district, the county commissioners' office, the regional planning office, the chamber of commerce, the local economic and community development group, and the senior leaders from the two and four year institutions. To date, outcomes from this group include a joint mission statement, a zoning overlay, and an initial draft of a 65-acre walkable community that includes both residential and retail opportunities, and the landing of a federal grant to be used for economic development planning process.

Summary

The main objective of this chapter was to present the mobilization cycle as a framework for understanding how data-gathering efforts exist inside of larger processes that must involve both campus and community stakeholders. Five phases – awareness raising, coalition building, data gathering, interpretation of results, and evidence-based action planning – were described theoretically, and then illustrated through a case example involving both a four year regional university and a co-located two year technical college.

7. PERSPECTIVES ON TOWN-GOWN LEADERSHIP

The main objective of this seventh chapter is to help readers gain insight into the processes by which campus and community leaders both conceptualize their roles and, as a result, take specific actions that are designed to strengthen town-gown relationships. As noted in the introduction of this book, the development of an optimal town-gown relationship is a full contact sport that requires continuous participation and maximum effort on the part of both campus and community leaders.

Scholarship focused on the role of the university president typically has included at least some mention of the need to attend to community relationships. For instance, in her 2012 book *"On Being Presidential: A Guide for College and University Leaders,"* Susan Resneck Pierce pointed out that presidential involvement with the local community presents both opportunities and risks. In order to provide a sense of how potential rewards versus costs can be weighed by university leaders, Pierce posed questions for presidents to ponder when considering initial (or greater) involvement in community partnerships. Interestingly, many of these questions seem "lopsided" in that they focused attention so heavily on whether or not *campus* needs were being met, echoing one of the major criticisms repeatedly lodged against university involvement in the community; that is, you only come to us when you want something for yourself. That said, "improved town-gown relationships" was in fact present on the list of issues for presidential deliberation generated by Pierce.

Weill's (2009) description of the president's role in developing positive town-gown interactions seemed a bit more balanced in terms of laying out the costs and benefits for *both* campus and community. As well, this journal article provided case examples that illustrated some of the steps that a president needs to take in order to more effectively engage community constituents. The steps included actions related to the formation of a stakeholder committee, for example, and the identification of specific goals to be accomplished through the activities undertaken within the partnership.

In the present chapter, we begin with the thoughts and reflections of university presidents who self-identify as having participated in establishing and maintaining functional town-gown relationships during their terms of office. Next, these contemplations are augmented by the perspectives of city managers who have served in municipalities containing an institution of higher education. By examining both sides of the town-gown relationship from the highest levels of administration, it was hoped that a set of common themes might emerge that would provide some initial indications of "emerging best practices" for campus and community leaders, to be discussed in the following chapter.

Forty Thousand Feet Up: The Role of University Presidents

Four former university presidents agreed to participate in a confidential interview regarding their town-gown experiences. Anonymity was guaranteed in order to maximize the opportunity for the emeritus presidents (one had held the title of chancellor due to the specific organization of higher education institutions in that particular state) to speak freely about their experiences. That said, all four participants served as the senior administrators of some of the larger comprehensive research universities located in the United States.

The information gathering process followed a semi-structured interview format. While a standard set of questions were asked of each university president, each participant was encouraged to take the conversation wherever necessary in order to generate the fullest possible portrait of the role they played in developing and maintaining campus-community relationships. The contents of these interviews are collated below as aggregated responses, and follow the original question and answer format employed in the interviews.

Question: What if any experiences prior to your having assumed the role of president prepared you for working on town-gown relationship?

All four of the university presidents generally claimed to have had some meaningful experiences in building and maintaining town-gown relationships prior to having assumed the presidency. Having role models that had specifically dedicated time and effort to the development and maintenance of town-gown relationships – as well as comparing the activities of those positive role models to the actions of others who did not hold similar values – was an essential component for several individuals in terms of recognizing the importance of focusing on campus-community interaction.

"It struck me that although I respected my previous place of employment as an academic institution, it didn't serve the town or the campus very well to have the kind of strained town-gown relationship that made it more difficult for the campus to do some of the things it wanted to do. The town would then be preoccupied with things it shouldn't be preoccupied with so it wasn't a good relationship. However, I only recognized this when I saw the provost I began working for in my new institution actually trying to do things with the community."

Location of the campus seemed to matter in terms of the ways by which previous positions impacted learning about campus-community interaction, especially by creating opportunities to connect with specific community stakeholders on town-gown issues.

> *My experiences certainly took a step up when I took the job at (name of institution withheld). There I was meeting regularly with the mayor, and because the campus was located in the state capitol, I was meeting regularly with the governor, and many of the members of the legislature as well."*

Of course, having town-gown relationships specified within one's portfolio of responsibilities and duties was a major factor in building experience levels as well.

> *"Within my previous position, the development of town-gown relationships needed to be intentional, and you needed to be organized in order to track them and follow them. If you don't do that, they become episodic, and you move from crisis to crisis, and no one is building lines of communication."*

Question: Using the Optimal College Town Assessment typology as a reference point, what sort of town-gown relationship did you inherit at the start of your presidency?

Often as not, the presidents used the "traditional" town-gown type to describe the situation they inherited. That is, the relationship between campus and community was relatively low on effort, but at least somewhat higher on comfort levels, mostly due to a lack of interest in making connections between town and gown activities.

"I think I inherited something that was less than ideal... there was a kind of benign neglect on the part of the university with the town. I wouldn't say there was an all-out war between the two entities, but it certainly wasn't a relationship that was at the optimal point, despite the fact that there were a lot of things that I saw very soon that could be done between the town and the university that would really help both sides."

One president did state unequivocally that he had inherited a harmonious relationship.

"There was a town-gown committee that was already in place by the time that I arrived. That committee was the formalization of what had already been a very positive relationship between the university and the community."

Further probing questions indicated that some of the relationships might have been labeled more accurately as having contained devitalized and conflicted relationship characteristics. One president described low effort in combination with low comfort (in this case, high suspicion), and went on to describe how much more difficult it was to do something with the discomfort factor.

When there's a tradition of suspicion it's more difficult to overcome than just low effort. When it's just low effort you can simply put in greater effort. But when there's a tradition of suspicion there's always questions. What are you doing that

for? Is it really going to benefit us, or is it just for you?

The theme of "suspicion" arose in some of the comments made by other presidents as well.

"Probably the most significant area of concern that I inherited had to do with the

suspicion that was present around development. When the university had improved

its food services on campus, for instance, it was felt that it had affected the way that

students spent their money downtown."

Here is a another example that focused more specifically on distrust surrounding student housing issues.

"The relationships were pretty good at the start. But there was a little tension

around certain issues, like housing, where the university by virtue of previous

decisions that had been made was perceived to be unfairly competing with developers

and what they were trying to do."

The term exploitation was introduced by one former university president to describe this lack of comfort inside of the town-gown relationship.

"There is a tendency on both sides toward exploitation. And maybe this is not

unlike the marriage model as well. This is where the city sees the university as a

target of opportunity, especially in terms of economic gain. What do I mean by that?

Let's take as an example real estate development. Private developers would want that vacant property that was strategically located either within the university campus or adjacent to it. They would want to purchase that land on an anticipatory basis whereby in three to five years the university would need that property and buy it back for a much larger sum. In turn, the university began to be more forward looking and proactive ourselves, so we started buying up property before they could get to it or understanding what we would likely need five or ten years down the road."

None of these comments should be surprising to readers. As noted earlier in this book, these sorts of land use issues are responsible for much of the conflict and stress that develop within town-gown relationships. Of course, the other major culprit is student misbehavior, and this issue also arose during this portion of the interview.

"There was the sense that the university wasn't controlling its students. I think that was a very damaging aspect of the relationship I inherited."

Finally, it also should be pointed out that several of the universities represented by these former presidents had regional or branch campuses, and these presidents were mindful of the fact that the town-gown relationship could look very different at these locations.

"There is a multi-campus dimension to this, so that when we talk about community relations it's not just the relationship between the main campus and the community.

It's also the relationships between our regional campuses and their communities,

which hold quite a different set of challenges."

Question: Who were the community stakeholders that you worked with most effectively during your tenure as president, and which stakeholders proved to be more of a challenge?

Overall, the former presidents uniformly discussed their contact with the business community as being one of the most important components of the town-gown relationship. Often as not, their interaction occurred both directly and indirectly through the local chamber of commerce. Much of this activity involved economic development assistance, which could take many forms.

"You've got to open up a dialogue. I met with all of the developers. I met with all of the associations. I gave annual briefings to the chamber of commerce and stood for questions on any topic. I had a standing agreement with the business community. Anybody the community was bringing in from an economic development standpoint that was considering locating here, I would meet with them and talk about the advantages of our community and the potential collaborations that could occur with our university."

Other frequently mentioned types of economic development activities involved workforce development actions taken on behalf of local industries and support given to various media outlets (especially radio stations that were located on or near the campus). And in those instances where the university had a medical center, there was significant mention made of economic activities undertaken on the health care front.

One president noted that business owners and leaders of industries necessarily must be seen as holding multiple roles as they relate to the university, including their connection to politicians.

"I saw the business leaders through multiple lenses. They were in many cases alumni, they were in many cases employers, and they were in many cases donors. They wore multiple hats. In fact almost everyone in the community plays multiple roles. For example, you have a subset of the members of the community who are politicians. They are members of the state legislature, or town council, or are private citizens who have close connections to political leadership."

Student-focused efforts also were often a source of connections to the business community that presidents had some hand in setting up. New student orientations and welcome back activities were launched, for instance, and often included promotional events that linked students to local shops and restaurants.

The presidents also discussed their involvement in the development of various partnerships and affinity agreements with banks and related financial institutions that encouraged student purchases at local businesses, typically through the use of their student identification cards. In many cases, there were shared service agreements that also brought campus and community leaders together.

"Our fire services for the entire community are based on our campus. On a regular basis, we are negotiating between the city and the campus about who pays what for what. And the same thing is true of our transportation system. It's a joint effort that gets regularly renegotiated in terms of who pays for the new buses and what services are going to be offered. So it requires pretty regular dialogue between the two groups about matters of money, which of course can be tedious. And not easy, because you're always feeling like you're paying more than you should."

Another prominent component of the town-gown relationship that presidents raised in this portion of the interview concerned connections with local schools. Often as not, this came about due to the demand for the university to provide some sort of targeted assistance to poorly performing schools.

"We developed all kinds of partnerships with the local school districts. We had continual movement of student teachers going back and forth between our campus and the schools. Often, when we had spousal hire issues with faculty members we were recruiting, we could find placements for them in the local schools. Our faculty members continuously served as resources in schools for in-service days, and a lot of teachers came to us to work on graduate degrees in the college of education."

There also were more personal reasons for being involved in the local schools, of course.

> *"My children were in the local school system at the time. So meeting with teachers, going to PTA meetings and so forth, my wife and I were pretty involved in that. And symbolically that became really important in terms of erasing the lines between what was a campus issue and what was a community issue."*

Finally, presidents also all mentioned the importance of connecting with the non-profit community, which typically was handled through leadership on United Way campaigns and their presence on various governing boards for area agencies and organizations. There also were a variety of "signature events" that the presidents used as leverage to encourage greater community involvement by faculty, staff, and students.

> *"On Martin Luther King Day there was a very active effort to get our campus involved in efforts being undertaken by the non-profits. It was a day we would spend in the community, and we should have done that more often, but at least that one day a year we all were actively involved in stacking cans and loading and unloading trucks."*

Question: How did you create alignment among your leadership team in terms of emphasizing the importance of town-gown issues and coordinating activities designed to strengthen campus-community relationships?

One of the most prominent strategies for creating alignment reported by the presidents involved the appointment of a "point person" who has the authority to speak for the president on town-gown matters, and could facilitate rapid decision-making on areas of concern.

'The most important thing that I did is that I took a member of my senior staff, someone I trusted very much, and I made him the official representative of the university to the town. I didn't have time to do this myself, because there was too much else that I had to do. If you set this person at a fairly low level then they know that you aren't taking things very seriously and it isn't really important to you. If you set this person at a higher level, then you know that someone is really concerned about those things."

This was not seen as not a substitute for the president showing up for events, of course, as presidents asserted uniformly.

"Obviously I met with the people of the town myself. I met with the town manager and I went to events that were scheduled in the town, meeting with the town council, things like that. So it wasn't the case that I wasn't there."

In most cases, the point person had lots of other responsibilities beyond town-gown issues, and was often seen as coordinating overall university communications and/or the management of external constituencies (handling overall government relations, for instance). As well, ongoing coordination of town-gown activities with other senior staff members also was part of the point person's position description, especially in terms of synchronizing those activities that involved student interaction with the community.

One of the former presidents mentioned having a senior administrator with specific outreach and engagement responsibilities. While a part of the overall town-gown team for this university, however, this individual was not thought of as the primary driver of campus-community relationships due to other significant obligations in other areas. And for other presidents, at least some of the town-gown issues were being addressed at lower administrative levels.

"Many town-gown relationships were tended at a lower level of administration, particularly through the Office of Student Affairs, which had extensive relationships with the city. And the same was true of police and fire services. So they tended to be more functionally driven I believe than organizationally or structurally driven."

Another former president took a different stance, asserting that the responsibilities were not given to one or even a small group of administrators.

"There was not one person that I gave these responsibilities to. When there were certain issues that came up, different members of my administrative council would take the responsibility for that particular issue. Certain assignments were made and

certain people would follow up. It wasn't just one individual. Everybody had that as part of their responsibilities."

Question: How did you involve faculty in town-gown activities?

As noted above, some of the presidents mentioned specific faculty involvement in local school systems, largely due to requests for assistance to be given to poorly performing schools. Creating solutions to a variety of other social issues – crime, violence, and child abuse, for instance – also were mentioned as catalysts for faculty involvement in town-gown affairs. Interestingly, some presidents noted that this sort of community involvement had to be extended to greater distances beyond the immediate reach of the campus. This was the case when a "target problem" of interest to the faculty member was not present in the home community of the institution.

One president discussed the role that he played in setting a tone about what faculty members could expect in terms of support for their participation in town-gown affairs.

"It was publically stated in many of my early addresses and advanced through some of my key initiatives that community involvement would be a key priority of the university. Our promotion and tenure guidelines were revised to reflect that explicitly. Teaching, research, and public service and outreach is in those documents, and it's a section in everyone's promotion dossier."

Another president noted the pleasure he took in witnessing already existing positive town-gown interactions, something he said that he constantly expressed in his messages to encourage even more faculty involvement with community stakeholders.

"It was something I was very proud of and would brag about it in front of faculty groups. Oftentimes I would highlight some service learning activity that had a particularly significant impact on the life of an individual or a group of individuals. I would find myself attracted to presentations made by faculty and students about the work they were doing in the community. And if I was asked to speak, that was fine, too, but just being there to witness the reports that were being given was enough to reinforce the idea that this was important to me and important to the university. And the growth in service learning over the time I served as president was something we tracked. The numbers were just remarkable. And they escalated over time."

At the same time, however, all of the former presidents were well aware of the dynamic tension involved in faculty members balancing their responsibilities in the areas of teaching, research, and service. As such, the need for faculty to connect service efforts to their scholarship activities was something consistently noted in this section of the interview.

"When I look at a research university, my feeling is that if you are doing service

like that, then it should have something to do with your research activity. It shouldn't be seen as a substitute for research. So I don't know if I can be sympathetic to those who say that I've done all of this service, but I don't have any research."

One president also noted that faculty (and staff, for that matter) have a dual role to play in town-gown relationships. That is, they are both campus representatives and members of the community as a function of where they reside.

"One way to think about this is that your faculty and staff are themselves members of the community if they choose to think of themselves that way. Most of them in my experience tended not to think in community terms per se. That is, they had their own lives and their own academic relationships and they tended to be less involved in community activities. If anything, my role was to sensitize them to those opportunities to become more involved and active in the community."

Question: How did you involve students in town-gown activities?

This book has noted in a number of places that the "tip of the sword" in town-gown relationships is the student body. The presidents uniformly understood this to be the case, and their comments on the issue of student involvement in the community typically were couched in terms that recognized the emphasis on how student involvement drove community perceptions of the entire university, for better and for worse.

"Students are the most critical element in town-gown relationships, and they are the most difficult. They are temporary residents, and oftentimes they don't have the maturity levels. When you have problems with the town, it's usually not because of the faculty or staff. It's because of student misbehavior."

All of the former university presidents noted that service learning courses were available to students during their tenure. One president had been actively involved enough in encouraging service learning opportunities to comment on this type of connection to the community.

"One particular year, for example, there was a service learning class that spent the entire semester studying the downtown area. They were actively involved with the city council, and if fact were asked to take on some aspects of the study by city council members. In some ways that became a political football within the council, but the students stayed the course and said this is what we believe and this is what you should do. And as a result there were many decisions that were made in the community, and on the campus, for that matter, that were strongly influenced by the work that the students had done. And I'd like to think that those decisions got a little better.

Many other types of student-oriented activities counted as contributing toward improved campus-community interaction in the eyes of the former presidents.

> *"There's a range of town-gown activities that students were involved in. Our homecoming parade, for example, and lots of student volunteerism activities. Student government has a formal liaison with local government. There is a student-run legal council that deals with housing issues, and there's an off-campus housing student organization."*

Interestingly, after having moved on to another part of the interview, one former university president asked to go back to the topic of student involvement in town-gown relationships in order to discuss the ephemeral nature of working with and for students in this area.

> *"The thing you have to remember about students is that every year there is a changeover. Every year there are new students who weren't here for anything that happened the year before, and never heard the speeches. So, it has to be ongoing. You can't just think you've done it. Whatever you do, as far as the students are concerned, has to be re-upped every year."*

Question: Again using the Optimal College Town Assessment typology as a reference point, what was the nature of the town-gown relationship when you stepped down as president?

All of the former presidents reported significant movement toward more harmonious relationships by the end of their tenure.

> *"I wouldn't say that we succeeded in doing everything that we wanted to do, but certainly the relationships and the trust between the university and the town were at*

a much higher level."

The one president who claimed that he had inherited a harmonious relationship believed that his main responsibility was simply to maintain the relatively high quality town-gown interactions that were already occurring.

"I would like to say that I turned things around when I became president but that's simply not true. Anything I contributed was simply baby steps in the direction we were already going. So there was never anything that I had to fix. It was making sure that we kept the momentum going and never took it for granted. That it was something very precious, and my job was to make sure I didn't screw it up."

The number of years in the position seemed to be related to the degree to which more positive relationships ensued. In essence, longer terms yielded more harmonious tendencies.

"The role of the president is to create trust among a number of constituencies, particularly the faculty and the board of trustees within the university, but also trust within the business community, the immediate residential community, and frankly trust with the political and media networks. Quite honestly, over a number of years I think that's what we got right. I was lucky in that I became a president fairly early in my career, and I had a relatively long tenure as president. If you have that kind of continuity and longevity it's possible to nurture relationships that build trust in a way that you can't if you have someone in a leadership position maybe three to five years. A new person then comes in and you have to start all over

again."

Much of this movement toward improved relationships surrounded the improvement in how campus and community leaders interacted with one another over the years.

"As years went on the collaboration and conversation became much more focused. We started to look at the possibility of consolidating certain services such as fire protection. The university had a fire service alongside one in the community. Eventually we agreed to merge these services into a single, mutually coordinated operation. The same thing happened in terms of police services. We were constantly looking for ways to actively collaborate with one another."

One university president noted that in the end it all came down to giving and receiving respect.

"I think the main thing from the university's standpoint is to be respectful. It's easy I think for the president of a very large university with a multibillion dollar budget to try to look down their nose at the local small town community mayor or town council. Treating them with respect, including them in your orbit, so that at the very least you are telegraphing to them on a fairly regular basis that, yeah, we know you exist, and if you have any issues come talk to me. Or if I have any issues I'll come talk to you. So I had dinner with these folks, lunch with these folks, and we invited them to all of our social events."

Question: What are you most proud of in terms of your town-gown accomplishments, and what do you wish you could have done better?

This portion of the interview generated a balanced portfolio of "wins" and "losses" as discussed by the former presidents. On the one hand, as noted above, all of the participants felt positive about their impact on the overall town-gown relationship itself. In a summative statement, one president stated succinctly that "I think the most important thing that we were able to do is align the strategic interests of the community and those of the university." Even more briefly, another president quipped: "We set town-gown relationships on the right track." Another president was a bit more loquacious.

"What I guess I was most proud of was the degree to which town-gown relationships became an embedded part of our culture. To a degree that was true before, but now it has been cemented and it is celebrated. When people are asked what makes our university different than others, I think our faculty would say 'hey, we got a really great town-gown relationship going here.' Our students would even say that, I think."

There were a variety of regrets that also were expressed by the former presidents, and nowhere was that disappointment more acutely expressed than in the realm of student misbehavior, even as they expressed a sense of powerlessness to completely eradicate such issues.

"I sympathize with the town in terms of what they were objecting to. When I saw some of the students getting out of hand, I certainly wouldn't want those kinds of things happening in my neighborhood. It's difficult for me to say that we could have done things better. You know, when you have twenty thousand eighteen to twenty one year olds in one area and they get alcohol it's very difficult to stop that from happening.

Another president discussed something similar in terms of his disappointment and regret about not being able to do more to reduce student alcohol use.

"I guess the most tedious thing has to do with how you handle student alcohol consumption. There are businesses right near the edge of campus that make a living out of providing that. Maybe there was more that I could have done in terms of making sure that students were more protected. Whenever we would lose a student it would haunt me."

One president lamented his knowing only in hindsight that the path toward better town-gown relationships would have to pass through a civics education process that instilled in students a better sense of their obligations to the community within which they were getting their educations.

"I wish we could have done a better job in having the students have a more civil

attitude toward their surroundings. A civil consciousness, a recognition that they are living in a community and that they have obligations even though they are only temporary residents. All these kids come from neighborhoods where they live, but they treat the university differently, and they treat the surroundings of the university differently."

Finally, one of the former presidents had experiences that left him feeling somewhat cynical about the degree to which others actually valued significant action taken to address town-gown concerns.

"What I have learned about higher education unfortunately is that if you want to be safe as a leader then you are better off doing less than more. Because when you try to do more for the community you end up stepping on people's toes, and what they really want is something glitzy, rather than something that is substantive."

Question: If you could go back in time and talk to yourself when you were first starting out as a new president, what advice would you now give to yourself in terms of town-gown relationships?

For this final question, the full text of each of the former presidents responses is provided in unabridged fashion, as these direct quotes speak for themselves.

University President 1: *"Take them very seriously. Devote enough staff time to this. Make sure you understand the town needs and wants, and don't make assumptions about that. And although you're not going to sacrifice what you need and want, find those places where what you need and want overlaps with what the town needs and wants, and work very hard on those areas."*

University President 2: *"I might have devoted – even though I didn't have any more time, I was already doing hundred hour weeks – I could have squeezed out a little more time, spent a little more time with community leaders who were inclined to have a more suspicious view of the university and warm up to them. I remember a couple of them at the beginning who were so intense, so adversarial, and it didn't have to be that way."*

University President 3: *"I'd say get comfortable with them very early on. They won't take all of your time, they'll take a relatively minor fraction of your time. You don't live in isolation, you live in a broader environment, and it's certainly in the self-interest of the university to nurture those relationships as a way of constructing an environment in which the university can flourish. You can look at it more broadly in terms of the university's mission. That is, to improve, change and support society itself. You need to recognize that the community is your backyard and you need to have a constructive and positive situation there."*

University President 4: *"I think what I would tell myself is to be prepared to carve out more time than you think you are going to need to make those town-gown relationships stronger. It takes a lot of time and energy to get those relationships to where you will want them to be.*

The View from the Town

Four city managers (also known as city administrators) who have larger comprehensive research universities within their municipal boundaries also agreed to participate in a confidential interview. As with the presidents, the information gathering process followed a semi-structured interview format, and each participant was encouraged to take the conversation wherever necessary in order to generate the fullest possible portrait of the role they played in developing and maintaining campus-community relationships.

While most of the questions mirror those that were asked of the university presidents, a small number of items were edited to better capture the essential town-gown experiences of city managers. The contents of these interviews are collated below as aggregated responses, and follow the original question and answer format employed in the interviews.

Question: What prior experiences did you have in working with universities when you first became city manager of a college town?

The city managers had a range of experiences in town-gown relationships prior to assuming their administrative positions. One of the individuals walked onto the job with no previous experience in college town dynamics. Two city managers claimed one previous college town position in their backgrounds. The fourth city manager reported holding two previous positions in a college town prior to assuming their most recent

administrative responsibilities.

Question: Using the Optimal College Town Assessment typology as a reference point, what type of town-gown relationship did you inherit when you first started as a city manager?

One of the city managers reported that he had inherited a

harmonious relationship, while the remaining three individuals reported

walking into town-gown relationships that were more traditional by nature.

Here is an excerpt of what the one city manager said about the harmonious

relationship he inherited.

> *"There was already a strong relationship between the campus and the community by*
>
> *the time I arrived. What helped to really catapult this relationship to become even*
>
> *better was my appointment to the president's cabinet as the city representative. I*
>
> *learned a lot sitting on that cabinet, and I think that they in turn learned a lot*
>
> *about how to consider the community around them when major decisions needed to*
>
> *be made."*

In turn, an example is provided here about the traditional relationship that

another city manager described as inheriting.

> *"The university president and I started at about the same time. He was into*
>
> *building the university endowment, into expanding the international reach of the*
>
> *university, building relationships with his board of trustees, with donors, all that*

stuff. So we were not on the center of his radar screen. We were on his radar screen, but it was out on the periphery somewhere. And the university had just abandoned a largely symbolic initiative where they had consciously created touch points between the university and city administrations. That initiative subsequently had been described to me as an elaborate opportunity to talk problems to death. It never really captured the attention of university leadership, and it just kind of went away right before I came. It seemed to die a death of natural causes."

The third city manager had described difficulties within the municipality that had to be dealt with prior to dealing with town-gown issues.

"Twenty years ago, I don't know if I was brave or stupid. I stepped into a situation where our governing body was the conflicted relationship. Almost every vote was a 4-3 vote, and I thought I had to fix that before I fixed anything else. We had a tough first year, with seven governing members who were hardheaded to the point that there was a lack of civility in our meetings. We spent that first year getting those members to act like a governing body. I basically told that group that we could not hope to have good external relationships with the university if we could not get along together inside of our own building."

Question: Again using the Optimal College Town Assessment typology as a reference point, how have you witnessed changes in effort and comfort levels over the years you have served as a city manager?

All of the city managers reported witnessing changes in the

characteristics of the town-gown relationships across time. The one city manager with experience in multiple college town settings said this:

"In all three instances, no matter how good the interactions were already, I saw movement toward more harmonious relationships. All three improved not only their relationships with each other, but also their understanding that the relationships had to improve. The competition these universities are facing for both faculty and students is driving this willingness to cooperate with towns. No student or faculty moves to a university any more thinking hey I'll live my whole life inside these walls. So, students and faculty members are going to be shopping for communities that have a high quality of life. Not to mention the shrinking financial resources. Universities now have to use an economy of scale with their surrounding communities to lower their infrastructure costs while improving the quality of life."

One city manager reported vacillating movement toward and away from a more conflicted relationship as a result of the rising influence of neighborhood associations, which was seen as a direct response to complaints about student behavior.

"I would even go as far as to say that, depending on the issue at hand, the relationship can move right now between harmonious and conflicted. We have days and months where it's very harmonious and other times where it is very conflicted. It depends on the issue and what's going on at the time."

Another city manager noted that the trend toward greater interaction between the city and the university came as the result of more intense focus on student housing, which meant that the relationship moved from traditional to harmonious only after a period of conflict had been resolved around off-campus residential issues.

"We were in a more traditional relationship pre-2008, when things were relatively calm and stable. This was during the growth curve of high school graduates, so universities had choices and lots of resources. And for us, the city had a long history of accepting the plight – the blight – of off-campus housing. We hadn't yet reached the point where we said 'hey wait a minute, maybe we don't have to accept this as a fait accompli. We can do some things to keep single family neighborhoods together, to keep students from living in squalor.' I'd like to take some credit for challenging those things. We got the attention of the university in the midst of some riots that were happening in some off-campus student residential areas. Eventually they realized it was in their best interest to clean this up."

Another city manager noted that the change in town-gown relationships came as the direct result of the changeover in university presidents.

"When I wished to interact with the previous president, I was told that I had to make an appointment. That president's executive assistant would give me the choice of two or three days in the upcoming week or so. When the new president took over, he came to me, to

140

my office, and said that he understood that there may have been some problems in getting

together with the previous president. We talked for a while, and then he took out his

business card, and with a pen he wrote his personal cell phone on the back of the card,

telling me that I should feel free to call him anytime. I only had to use that phone number

once in fourteen years of doing business with him, but it sure felt good to have that

number in my hands."

Question: Who were the campus leaders that you interacted with most frequently, and how would you describe the level of importance they seemed to place on strengthening town-gown relationships?

The most frequently mentioned campus representatives were the senior administrators in charge of student life, public safety, and business and finance. The prevailing sentiment was that these individuals had the appropriate decision-making authority or otherwise could access the president quickly enough so as to maintain the momentum within various dialogues that were occurring around issues of central importance to both the campus and community. The city managers also claimed sufficient access to the presidents when needed, although it was clear in most instances that the presidents were not their main point of contact.

"We always had access to the president, although those interactions were not as

frequent. If there was a critical need we had the ability to make a phone call and

have an interaction with the president of the university directly."

Another city manager noted that access to multiple levels of campus administrators was a functional way of handling various town-gown issues.

"Eventually I began to work with a broader range of decision-makers beyond administrative vice presidents, including deans, the athletic director, student body president, faculty senate president, people like that. It provided an avenue where I didn't have to go to the president for something. I had personal relationships with the decision makers in the more direct levels of the areas in which I needed help."

One city manager reported that the ascension of a president from within the ranks of the university created an opportunity for meaningful and regularly scheduled meetings that were personally attended by that president.

"The new president, having lived in the community and having been with the university for many years, it mattered to her. It wasn't just symbolic. We had quarterly meetings between the president's staff and city leadership, with printed agendas. It wasn't just show and tell, we got at economic development, and housing, and police and community relations. The tough issues. And we kept at them with the expectation that, in three months, there was going to be progress made on these issues. The president was going to hold her people accountable for progress, and she was going to hold me and my people accountable as well. This compared well to what I have heard from my city manager colleagues, who typically report having a particular vice president assigned to them as a primary point of linkage between the

campus and the community."

The issue of equality between university presidents and city managers came up repeatedly, and was cited as one of the reasons why access to the president was indeterminate at times. One city manager described the relationship in this manner.

"Structurally, the city manager and the university president are equals. But they're not really. The university president is a CEO of a multibillion dollar enterprise. Even the biggest cities pale in comparison to these universities in terms of resources at their disposal. And so I'm not sure that university presidents always see themselves as the equal of the city manager."

Question: Who were the community stakeholders that seemed to work most effectively on town-gown issues with you, and which stakeholders proved to be more of a challenge?

There was fairly uniform agreement among the city managers that members of the business community were most actively involved in town-gown relationships.

"The business community of course is very, very influential. Along with the Chamber of Commerce, business leaders played prominent roles on the town-gown advisory committee. Working through the city, they most often were able to lobby in order to make their interests known to the university. And there was a very strong community foundation that also played an active role in mediating relationships between the city and

the university. And of course the foundation's board members were almost all business owners from the community."

The business of bar ownership drew particular attention from several of the city managers in their discussions of collaborating partners.

"The bar owners didn't partner with the city in an organized manner so much because they thought it was the right thing to do, you know, to get at student drinking as a behavioral issue. We made it clear that, if you weren't seen as being on our team and then you had problems of some sort, you were going to get treated differently than those bar owners who would play. So bar owners came to the table, but not willingly. They were arm-twisted."

Interestingly, changes in leadership were noted as playing a chilling effect on relationships between the university and the business community.

"The business community is not as involved with the university now as it was when I started as city manager. Due to changes in personnel, some of those relationships between the town and university have lessened. There are still some things that happen, but I don't think the active roles that had been taken before to undertake joint economic development projects are quite as strong now as they were previously. And it's on both sides of the street. The university has gone through major changes in key administrative positions and the downtown leadership group has gone through similar changes. And the personal relationships just aren't what they were

before. I'm not saying they won't develop in the future, but at this moment in time they are not as strong as they once were."

Law enforcement was also a common focal point for the city managers in terms of important stakeholders.

"We saw a great set of relationships develop around law enforcement, and it may be the case that these great relationships spread to other relationships. Interestingly, this came about in the face of some previous difficulties. At one point, the university was going to host a big rock concert in their football stadium. And the community and the police department didn't know anything about this until the day the concert was announced in the newspaper. Which meant you were going to have 50,000 people coming in for a late night concert in a town that had never experienced such an event. And it really opened people's eyes to the idea that the campus and community needed to start talking. The police department became one of the first and most important focal points of that town-gown discussion."

In one instance, the intersection of law enforcement and local clergy received mention, again in response to prior negative events that triggered the need for something different to happen.

"Over the past year, some issues around race relations and law enforcement have arisen because of the national landscape. We have had a somewhat closer relationship and have done some things differently with clergy, especially a pastor of one of the African

American churches here. We've facilitated conversations involving university students and university employees who live in town, focusing on the relationships between the African American community and the police."

One city manager expressed the opinion that local government was the most consistent point of contact between the university and the community, with all other community partners only sporadically becoming involved in the development and maintenance of town-gown relationships.

"I don't know who I would point to as a consistent partner. I would perhaps point to the occasional business leader, in part to either protect a real estate investment, or some other investment, but not to roll up their sleeves to tackle problems for any altruistic reasons. It would be hard for me to identify a non-governmental interest. The schools occasionally, but again out of self-interest, because of how schools are funded. It was a city sometimes in partnership with the university, and sometimes in conflict with the university. It was also sometimes a city versus a landlord, and a city versus a bar owner, and I use the term versus consciously."

Question: What was the general sense that you had about faculty member investment in the community?

The overall sentiments expressed by the city managers were positive in their orientation toward faculty members.

"Faculty members were seen in a positive light. Not perfect, but very positive. Because many faculty members were active in the community as residents, they often

came across as knowing more about things than they really do. For instance, a professor of philosophy sitting on a regional planning commission who believes they are also experts in land use and engineering and everything else. But overall the community members appreciate the involvement and the interaction. Because faculty member involvement on boards and non-profit organizations and the churches gives community members access to information from inside the walls of the university."

One city manager was well-versed in the service learning and outreach and engagement scholarship efforts that had been undertaken by faculty members in his community.

"For the past several years, there have been some new relationships that we have enjoyed with faculty members on engaged learning and engaged scholarship projects. We've worked fairly closely with a number of faculty members to create experiential opportunities for students to be involved in projects that directly benefit the community. So that has been an evolving process for us lately."

Another city manager noted that faculty members who also were community residents could serve as some of the biggest antagonists of the town's relationship with the university.

"To some extent, some of the most difficult relationships have been between faculty members acting as residents in their relationship with the university versus their employment role. So when we have conflict, sometimes the conflict is being driven by

the faculty and staff who work for the university. And that happens not

infrequently."

One city manager very specifically noted the dual role that faculty members played on both the campus and the community.

"The community saw the faculty members in a positive light, as ambassadors of the

city on campus. Many of these faculty members lived in areas that were very close to

the university grounds. Even in some of the neighborhoods that some people

characterized as the demilitarized zones, that boundary between chaos and idyllic

little college town neighborhoods. They were important because they lived it, much

more so than faculty who had chosen to live more of a suburban lifestyle. Those that

lived it had a great credibility, they had skin in the game, a lot at stake, and they

were highly regarded. And we would go to them, because we knew they had a voice

on campus."

Question: What was the community's take on students from the campus? Was it predominantly negative, or positive, or did it depend?

Every city manager agreed that the relationship between the community and the university's student body was multifaceted and therefore did not lend itself to an easy answer to questions about the positive or negative impact of students.

"The relationship is extraordinarily complex. I think that it depends. It depends

on who is living next door to you this year. It depends on whether or not there are factors in the community that positively or negatively impact perceptions. In general the relationship that we have with students is positive, and most people value that as positive, but there are some extraordinarily negative experiences that tend to color the greater conversation about students in general. It becomes almost a sort of sliding scale."

As implied in the quote above, a great deal of the complexity surrounds the ephemeral nature of the interactions between campus and community representatives, including most importantly the presence or absence of negative events.

"It's so complex, and it changes daily. All that needs to happen is one bad incident with students, and the relationship can change a hundred and eighty degrees. A lot of times something bad happens and it separates the community versus the students. But sometimes something really bad happens to a student and really quickly we all become one big family. You just don't know which way it's going to go."

One city manager heaped great praise on the efforts undertaken by the university president to create opportunities for students to become vitally engaged in the community.

"Our university president wanted his students to become university stewards, and he continually pushed the idea that you were privileged to go to college. He said that there are folks in your life that help you get to where you want to go in your life,

and because of that you have a responsibility to give back. And he really pushed student service in the community and volunteering at non-profit agencies."

City managers also spoke to the issue of geographical location playing a role in perceptions.

"Relationships are extremely dependent on where you live. If you surveyed people who lived south of the campus you would get very different answers than if you asked people who lived north of the campus. And if you live near a fraternity you are going to have a very different reaction to students than if you didn't live near a fraternity."

The type of neighborhood in which students live also plays a role in determining the community's perceptions.

"The community immediately surrounding the campus is not very affluent, not very high quality of life, so the students can blend in very, very easily. Where there are other areas that are even more impoverished, the students are not known for bringing up the quality of life there."

One city manager also noted that the particular composition of student residents also could pay an important role in determining the ways that students were perceived by the community.

"There was a monoculture of sophomore boys living in one particular area that

seemed to be creating most of the problems in the neighborhoods. And they gravitated to this area precisely because of the main issues: there were lots of loud parties, it was easy to get unrestricted amounts of alcohol, there were lots of disturbances, and therefore it was the cool place to be, you know."

At the end of the day, however, as one city manager noted, people had consciously made a decision to live in a college town, which meant that on the whole they had to realize what they were getting themselves into as a resident.

"There was a ton of sentiment that people lived in a college town for a reason. They liked being around young people. They were viewed as the ingredients of vibrancy, you know, that they looked for when they settled on a place to live. People who lived among the college students liked the fact that new people were always moving in next door. And they knew that this required a higher level of attention on their parts. They would bake cookies, take them to the new student residents, and say 'hey these are sort of the ethics we live by in the neighborhood. We're going to help you if you need it. And if you have loud parties, give us a phone number that we can use if you're disturbing sleeping children, for instance.' As a result, a good number of people saw the students as positive."

Question: What are you most proud of in terms of your town-gown accomplishments, and what do you wish you could have done better?

Similar to the responses given by the university presidents reported above, this portion of the interview yielded a mixture of "wins" and "losses" as discussed by the city managers. All of the participants were able to describe examples of the positive impact that their efforts had on the overall town-gown relationship itself.

"Without doubt I'm most proud of the creation of the town-gown committee. It's amazing to me that it hadn't been created before I got there. The ability to work with the campus and community leaders who saw the bigger picture, being a part of that kind of growth, was amazing."

A second city manager focused on progress made around public safety issues.

"We have some had some real and substantive partnerships develop around law enforcement and community relationships, especially in the area of the university's contribution to neighborhood policing efforts."

A third city manager discussed success in terms of perseverance.

"It's been enduring, that there hasn't been a time when people decided to just walk away. Both sides kept coming back for more. The town and the campus. I'm most proud of that, which is a cultural thing, right. I could point to this project or that program, but I

would say more that it was changing the culture so that people didn't give up on one another, they kept plugging away."

On the other hand, there were plenty of examples of unfinished business that the city managers wished that they had resolved at the time of these interviews. For instance, the need to develop more equitable financial models was specifically mentioned by several city managers:

"I think one of the key things I wish we had done better, that to this day we are still striving to do better, is to build a better financial model where the university's overall impact as a tax exempt entity and its economic impact on the community is better managed. I think we have had some success there but not enough. We struggle as a small community with a large university that is tax exempt and with a large number of low income residents as a result of student residences. It's not that they don't have pocket money to spend but they aren't earning income to help sustain the community. We haven't done enough to build a model that have some revenue sharing components that reflect those facts."

This was echoed by another city manager who noted that, while the town-gown interactions definitely had trended toward a more harmonious relationship, it was always going to be the case that the municipality wanted more out of the university than the other way around.

"It's typically the case that you hear people from the university say things like

We don't have money to give to you, but we have human capital. So why don't we put the brains of the university to work for the city.' Cynically, I think to myself that's all well and good. But can those brains come with some money. Solving problems require more than human capital. I think it's a common theme among city managers. Because a part of this is a physical planning function. How does the city keep its balance in terms of the economic mix, the housing mix."

Question: If you could go back in time and talk to yourself when you were first starting out as a city manager, what advice would you now give to yourself in terms of town-gown relationships?

In parallel with the final question asked of the former university presidents reported above, the city managers' responses to this last item are provided here in unabridged fashion.

City manager 1: *"I think we have had good relationships and I have been effective at building strong relationships with important people at the university. I think maybe I could have done more to broaden that relationship base to include a bigger part of that university in ways that would have been more important and more meaningful in the long run. And more sustainable. I think one of the lessons I have learned more recently is that as people change, relationships change. Building those deeper roots that institutionalize relationships so that they can survive changes in personnel is key."*

City manager 2: *"Build personal relationships. I used to just get the facts down, be able to prove why something is a good thing and try to sell it. Now, as I've gotten older, I believe that you can only sell something if you've got a good relationship with the person you are trying to sell it to. Then it's much easier because you have that trust, front and center, and the rest just becomes semantics to prove that it's feasible. I think a lot of college towns fall short because they treat everything on a case by case basis and let it rise or fall on its own merits. I think they lose a lot of opportunity doing that instead of having a more family oriented relationship. I would go back and build relationships more than what I did in the early years."*

City manager 3: *"Good town-gown relationships are bred out of persistence. And patience. These institutions have been there a long time and these cities have been there a long time. It's only those people on both sides of the town-gown relationships who make a difference. Too many city managers and too many university leaders are too content with not engaging with each other. To use the marriage analogy, how many marriages end up in separate bedrooms, taking separate vacations, even if you're not divorced. Too many people become comfortable with that."*

City manager 4: *"In terms of advice, I consciously look for ways to get my governing body inserted into an issue that has to do with the university. In other words, if there is a project or if there is a program or something else going on, I try to make sure that we have a council representative who is available to participate. Usually what we will do is ask for a volunteer from our governing body. You have to be very intentional about having a presence everywhere you can."*

Corroborating Information

The interview material presented earlier in this chapter represents the experiences and viewpoints of a small selection of university presidents. That said, there are other breadcrumbs that can be followed as we aspire to learn more about how senior university leaders conceptualize the role that they play in developing healthy town-gown relationships. One rather significant resource in this regard is a 2006 book entitled *Leadership in Higher Education* that was compiled by Francis Lawrence, the former president of Rutgers University. This book contains material culled from his interviews with twelve university presidents, all of whom were asked to respond to a number of important questions, including one that requested commentary on the role of the university within the communities that surrounded their campuses. A sampling of those replies below illuminate additional issues that can and should become the focus of future efforts to better understand town-gown relationships from the standpoint of senior administrators in higher education settings.

Every university president interviewed by Francis Lawrence underscored the importance of town-gown issues in one way or another. For instance, Mary Sue Coleman, former president of both the University of Iowa and the University of Michigan, argued that an ongoing campus-community dialogue was an essential component of the interdependent nature of the town-gown relationship.

"We don't always agree because sometimes we have differing needs and differing expectations, but I think the communication is absolutely critical because we are totally dependent on each other. The university is dependent on having a nice city. The town is dependent on us to draw people here."

Shirley Jackson, the longstanding president of the Rennselaer Polytechnic Institute, pointed out that sometimes universities have to help their community partners with the most mundane of projects in order to get along well.

"We have things ranging from neighborhood revitalization programs, where we actually give people grants to fix up their homes or to address safety or code violation issues, to where we have actually done streetscape improvements putting in new signal lights, sidewalks, and lighting."

At the same time, managing the reciprocal nature of town-gown relationships is made more difficult when there are imbalances in the power and influence of the campus and community. Robert Berdahl, former president of both the University of Texas at Austin and the University of California at Berkeley, argued that the size of the university in relation to the municipality will greatly influence the positive or negative valence of the relationship. Whereas UT Austin was a big university in a big city, he noted, Berkeley was a big university in a very small town. As a result, Berdahl portrays Berkeley as a "very big elephant in a little place and is resented."

Similar thinking regarding size differences was expressed by Shirley Kenny, past president of Stony Brook University.

"The locals have never realized that their economy is based on Stony Brook. We are the largest single-site employer in Suffolk County, which has about a million and a half people. They have never taken account of the fact that their neighbors teach at the university and that the university is a great asset to them. Instead, it has always been resented. That has meant a very different kind of connecting with the community. So we connect with civic groups and with the school systems."

Difficulties also arise when presidents are not attuned to the importance of town-gown relationships. In a very candid moment, William (Brit) Kirwan, former president of both The Ohio State University and the University of Maryland, admitted as much.

"When I became president, I didn't really understand the importance of external relations or how much time needs to be devoted to this area. By the time I left the University of Maryland, we had launched a successful capital campaign, developed a government relations program, reinvigorated our alumni operations, and begun

serious marketing efforts. You might say I'd gotten religion on the subject."

Using a slightly more granular focus, Myles Brand, former president of both the University of Oregon and Indiana University, asserted that the most important variable in the success of town-gown relationships is the economic well-being of the state.

"A public university engaged in the economy of the state will create a greater partnership with elected officials and business leaders as well as helping itself."

Similar sentiments were expressed by Molly Corbett Broad, former president of the University of North Carolina, who highlighted the significance of working with legislators when she noted that "the general assembly is our banker. They provide the resources."

David Ward, former president of the University of Wisconsin at Madison, shared his thoughts on the complex relationships that exist between a university and the business community, with special emphasis on leveraging alumni connections.

"The relationship with the business community was a complicated one, but on the whole a very positive one. I tended to work through the UW alumni association and the UW foundation to reach the business community in order to focus on people who already had some connection and loyalty to Madison."

Former president of MIT, Charles Vest, also focused on the economic relationship between campus and community. "We have helped to build the economy of the city and its future together." However, at the same time he also underscored the importance of recognizing public service. Noting that he and his wife gave out an annual community service award to a member of both the campus and the community, Vest stated that:

"I would have never believed how much good will this elicited. The recognition of people who do great things in public service to the community and the sense it engenders of all being in it together have been extremely important."

John Casteen, former president of both the University of Connecticut and the University of Virginia, focused his campus-community interaction discussion on the importance of raising the bar regarding academic performance when he said that "public flagship universities must set the standards, especially with regard to what is taught in the schools." This was echoed by Nils Hasselmo, former president of the University of Minnesota, who discussed the need to balance the demand for educational excellence with the perception that a higher education degree is accessible.

"I think some of the things were possible to do because I was out on the hustings with the grassroots people often enough for them to say, 'Well, you know he's raising these admissions requirements, but he isn't necessarily a bad guy because he's out there talking to us.' And of course I loved doing it, too... I liked the people

I talked to, even when we disagreed."

That said, Norman Francis, former president of Xavier University in New Orleans, cautioned that requests for help from the community, especially from the educational system, can be fraught with difficulties.

"But we are pressured sometimes to do things we are not capable of doing... I said from day one that Xavier could not take over failing schools. Our department of education is small; I don't have people who I can assign to run a school. If I took a school over, I would have to go out and hire people to do it and, once that happens, it's no longer Xavier running that school."

Summary

The contents of this seventh chapter speak for themselves. We began this section of the book with the transcribed responses of former university presidents to the questions raised in their semi-structured interviews, followed by the responses of city managers to similar queries asking about the "community" side of the town-gown equation. It should be remembered that these particular presidents and city administrators were selected on the basis of their having been "known commodities" in terms of their investment in town-gown relationships. Therefore, in at least some respects they should be considered the "cream of the crop," and as such are not necessarily representative of senior leaders found in most campus and community settings.

Of course, generalizability was not the primary objective of this chapter. Instead, the main goal was to center attention on the development of "intentional leadership" within town-gown relationships, a theme that readers hopefully cannot help but notice in the various descriptions given by university presidents and city administrators regarding the actions they have undertaken to establish and maintain healthy campus-community connections.

Further, the additional information gleaned from Lawrence's book should make it clear that university presidents across the board accept the fact that they play a pivotal role in the establishment and maintenance of effective town-gown relationships. When we couple that line of thinking with the contents of interviews conducted with city managers discussed above, we see that both campus and community leaders have a determining part to play in the relative health and well-being of campus-community interactions.

8. TOWN-GOWN LEADERSHIP IN ACTION

The main objective of this eighth chapter of the book is to expand attention paid to the development of "intentional leadership" within town-gown relationships, a viewpoint that places primary emphasis on the critical role that senior university and municipal leaders play in establishing and maintaining healthy campus-community connections. We begin with an update of the town-gown relationship that I have been affiliated with as the senior administrator of a Big 10 regional campus, which served as the case example of the devitalized relationship in the fourth chapter of this book. This narrative is followed by the verbatim transcription of an interview conducted with E. Gordon Gee, who arguably has accumulated a more diverse set of town-gown experiences than any other living university president.

Because I had been doing so much work on town-gown relations over the course of my term as the senior administrator of the Ohio State Mansfield campus, I decided to go beyond the historical information in order to create a more up-to-date portrait of the situation that my campus and our surrounding communities experienced with one another since the time the original article was written and published in the *Innovative Higher Education* journal.

I made the choice to extend my chronicle here because I believe that this sort of updated information will provide readers with a magnified glimpse of the significant impact that campus and community leaders can have on the course of town-gown relationships. As well, the structure of this narrative reflects the framework of the questions I posed to campus and community leaders (as reported in the seventh chapter of this book) regarding the role that senior administrators play in the development and maintenance of healthy town-gown relationships.

Leadership Contribution Update: Mansfield Reengaged

By the time that I took the reins as Ohio State Mansfield's senior administrator in January of 2011, the public relations damage to my campus related to the loss of the nursing program (as described in the second chapter of this book) largely was complete. Parenthetically, however, the economic reverberations of those decisions were still being felt by Ohio State Mansfield for the first two years of my term in the form of rapidly declining enrollment numbers. In essence, the relatively large number of nursing students (approximately 15% of our total student body) whose general education requirements previously were being taken care of by our campus now were enrolled as full time students at the private university that had taken over the hospital's training program. Regrettably, the tough decisions about how to "right size" the budget in light of these enrollment declines had not been made prior to my arrival.

As a result, the need to stop the budgetary bleeding had to be reversed as soon as possible. Reducing our operating budget to match the lower enrollment figures was the short term solution, of course, and as a result I ended up cutting about $100,000 a month during the first two and a half years of my serving as the senior administrator of this campus. There simply was no way that the campus could handle a $2.5 million dollar cut all at once, so the budget reductions had to be slow, deliberate, and consistent.

However, the longer term response to the enrollment decline had to involve the construction of residential housing for students in order to attract and retain students from greater geographical distances, which of course is the story that I told at the beginning of this book. Although not all campuses can grow their way out of financial difficulties, in our case we knew that there was pent up demand for access to the Ohio State brand, especially in our catchment areas of North Central and Northeast Ohio.

To examine the intentional leadership efforts that were on display throughout this process of regrouping and reorientation, we will use the student housing project and related economic development efforts as the main backdrop against which the actions taken by campus and community leaders can be most properly viewed. As will be seen throughout the remainder of this section of the book, nothing less than a complete team effort from leaders on both sides of the town-gown equation was going to create the opportunity for student housing to be built. It was always, through both thick and thin, an intentional and collaborative leadership team effort amongst the main players.

It should be noted here that the residential project was the necessary and sufficient reason for this particular constellation of campus and community leaders to join forces on a variety of larger economic development issues. The campus needed to grow (at least back to its former enrollment size), and the surrounding communities were in desperate need of an economic shot in the arm that could be created by the residential and retail development that would surround an emergent Campus District. In situations faced by other campuses and communities – and this cannot be stated too forcefully – issues and concerns beyond student housing can and should become the focal point for town-gown partnerships to be developed and maintained.

The impact of the senior administrative team

A number of fortuitous events were conspiring to bring a top shelf leadership team together. On campus, my facilities supervisor indicated a desire to move into the position of campus project manager in order to oversee all on-campus and off-campus planning and operations initiatives. This role transition served to create alignment among my leadership team in terms of emphasizing the importance of town-gown issues while concurrently providing a single point of contact for coordinating activities designed to strengthen campus-community relationships. In addition, my Director of Student Life became the go-to person for all of the issues that began to spring up around our transition from a largely commuter campus to a more substantially residential one. While special attention was directed toward the need for this individual to become a liaison to the off-campus student housing facility, our Student Life Director also had helped to oversee a number of student-focused activities over the years (using both on-campus and at off-campus locations) that involved significant contact with community members. This had resulted in a significant amount of good will inside of the community that we could bank on throughout the planning process.

The impact of faculty members

Faculty members wielded their greatest influence directly through coursework that was conducted both in the classroom and out in the communities surrounding our campus. By far, the most significant impact was seen in the service learning courses that increasingly began to be taught by faculty in various disciplines. While these course offerings eventually involved faculty representatives in fields as disparate as English and Geography, the main concentration of work occurred in two areas that had historical ties to the community: education and the social sciences.

Service learning offerings from our education faculty members typically were tied directly to our teacher preparation program. Somewhat differently, our social science faculty members – including most specifically Psychology, Sociology, and Social Work – routinely offered service learning opportunities that could be tied to each of those discipline's demands for internship experiences in the community. Regardless of the specific discipline represented by a given faculty member offering the service learning class, this type of coursework was designed to provide students with a meaningful connection to community residents, employers, and resources in a manner that "brought to life" the teaching and learning efforts being conducted inside of the classroom.

Of course, faculty members also had more indirect impacts on town-gown relationships outside of their teaching and service responsibilities, especially the ones who resided in closer proximity to the campus. In general, community members highly valued the notion that faculty members were living in their midst as fellow citizens. At the same time, however, there was the occasional faculty member whose interactions with some prominent members of the community seemed to taint the more affirmative impressions that residential faculty typically generated. Hence, there was a decidedly mixed bag of positive and not-so-positive relationships that had to be negotiated along the way.

Interestingly, our survey efforts with community members also shed further important light on the topic of faculty involvement in the community. In response to the open-ended qualitative question (discussed at length in chapters 5 and 6) about how the campus could improve its relationship with the community, one resident shared a concern that we were overstating the impact of faculty members who were living in neighborhood areas near campus. This individual reported that one Ohio State faculty member – who happened to be their next door neighbor – was involved in a great number of volunteer efforts in the community through the church they both belonged to in town. That should not be counted as Ohio State involvement, the resident went on to explain in their written response to this survey item. That was reckoned to be part and parcel of that faculty member's obligations as a member of that church. If Ohio State wanted this sort of activity to "count" as a university contribution, this resident continued, then that faculty member should invite other faculty members who were not part of that church to participate in those same volunteer activities. Oh yes, the citizen continued, and they all needed to wear their Ohio State gear at those events in order to be properly recognized as representing the university.

The impact of students and alumni

In some important ways, the impact of students is predicated on the response immediately preceding this one regarding faculty member emphasis on service learning. Students who participated in such coursework became enormously influential on the community's perceptions of our campus, of course. At the same time, however, student involvement in a variety of additional (and less formal) activities in the community also became more significant over time. This included their having served in a volunteer capacity for any number of well-known community philanthropic projects, as well as assisting as campus ambassadors during campus outreach and engagement initiatives in the community.

In turn, the student representative from our local board of trustees (who also chaired the student advisory board to the dean) agreed to serve as a champion for even greater student involvement in the community. This resulted in a series of discussions with various student groups about further student involvement in a wide range of on-campus and off-campus issues. Many of these topics – including but not limited to the availability of internships and cooperative experiences, relationships between our student life office and off-campus housing representatives, and contact with local police and public safety officials – are now established check-in points that have become embedded in the ongoing dialogue between my office and our students when we meet as a group.

Finally, students from the Columbus campus also were responsible for developing a countywide economic development plan for Richland County, Ohio. Our campus had been approached by the local economic development group to see if we could harness some of the brainpower on the Columbus campus in order to help create a countywide economic development plan. Fortunately, contacts in the college of business as well as in the city and regional planning department were only too eager to have their students "adopt" the county as a class project focus.

Through these efforts, the county received a state of the art economic development plan for a relatively small amount of money (most of which was used to pay student costs associated with travel back and forth from the Columbus campus). This is the brilliance of having conceptualized The Ohio State University as "six campuses, one university," an idea that was developed and promoted by former Ohio State President Gordon Gee (to be discussed at greater length below). It literally did not matter what geographical location you held at any given point in time, according to Dr. Gee. Extrapolated to our situation, what mattered was that our university's students were available to provide assistance in their area of expertise for communities throughout Ohio that were in need of such help.

In the meantime, alumni of the university living in the immediate area also became great supporters of the campus's efforts to improve relationships with the community. A significant number of those alumni became much more vocal in their support of these efforts, both individually and in the organized alumni groups that were active in the area. While the majority of these community residents had graduated from the Columbus campus, many of them had gotten their start on the Mansfield regional campus. As part of a capital campaign that was launched several years ago, particularly powerful testimonials were given by several alumni living in the area who proclaimed that, but for presence of the Ohio State Mansfield campus, they would not have had the opportunity to go to college. This advocacy effort was further extended through the provision of vocal support for the Campus District initiative.

The impact of governing board members

The role of the Ohio State Mansfield Advisory Board (serving at the pleasure of the Provost in an advisory capacity to the Dean) is to provide community support and direction to the campus. The Mansfield Board is comprised of nine individuals who are deemed to be leaders of the community, and represent a variety of profession positions, backgrounds, and residential locations throughout the service area of the campus. Historically, board members provide assistance in maintaining key relationships with community stakeholders, serve as an advocate with state and local governing bodies, and offer general guidance on issues and concerns that impact the campus.

Mansfield Board members most often worked to enhance town-gown relationships through one-on-one contacts with various constituents. In addition, as the off-campus student housing project began and the concept of the Campus District took hold, these exchanges with community members grew in frequency and importance. This was especially noticeable when matters such as water and sewer agreements came before the city councils of Mansfield and Ontario. Board members were present at council meetings to register their support for Campus District initiatives as both campus representatives and as residents of the community. They also provided a significant amount of behind the scene support through more personalized one-on-one lobbying efforts in between council meetings.

Early on in my tenure, I also sought to create a Mansfield Board Alumni Group, consisting of all former members of the advisory board. Almost all of these individuals still lived in the area, and the vast majority remained active in the social and political fabric of the community. As a result, town-gown relationships were quietly but significantly impacted by the advocacy efforts of these citizens over time.

Ironically, for all that Mansfield Board members did for the campus over the years, they did not leave an indelible impression on the community at large. In fact, the data generated in the community survey conducted by Ohio State Mansfield indicated that board members were the least well-known representatives of the campus. In response to this information, Mansfield Board members began to create a strategic plan for increasing their visibility and identity in the community. At present, plans are being finalized that will lead to the development of at least one "signature project" highlighting the identity of board members and their many contributions to the well-being of the campus and community.

The impact of business and industry leaders

One of the major criticisms historically lodged against the Ohio State Mansfield campus was about being out of touch with local community wants and needs, and especially those of the business community. I found out just how salient an issue this was when a consultant was hired to conduct a feasibility study just prior to launching our capital campaign effort in 2012. The subsequent report indicated that we were seen as being largely unresponsive to the needs of the local economy according to business and industry leaders who participated in the interview process. Over and over again, statements were made comparing us to our co-located technical college partner in an unfavorable manner. As in: why can't you be more like the technical college?

Ironically, the disparagement we heard from business leaders in the feasibility study report were loud echoes of the same sentiments expressed over a decade earlier. Perusing the campus archives for some historical information about the founding of our campus, my executive assistant happened to come across a feasibility study that was conducted prior to the 1993 capital campaign effort. I was discouraged by what I read in this report, to say the least. Same statements, different year (different century, actually). I realized that something had to be done, and quickly, if we were to have any hope of successfully raising money for the campus.

As luck would have it, at exactly the same time we were launching our feasibility study, the state of Ohio was soliciting proposals for internship programs that would better connect institutions of higher learning to the needs of the business community. In partnership with our co-located technical college, the Ohio State Columbus campus, and a local community college serving the greater Columbus metropolitan area, we were successful in landing a grant that provided the initial funding for what became known as our business and industry internship program. Within the first year alone, this program was responsible for having placed over 50 students in companies throughout our service area. As a result, many local business owners stepped forward to contribute to this specific fund, and our capital campaign efforts rather easily raised the $500,000 that we had sought as an endowment to continue supporting this initiative.

As noted above, we also had been approached by the local economic development group to help the county with its strategic planning efforts regarding the growth of the local economy. The ensuing student-generated economic development plan included ample documentation that supported the creation of a Campus District surrounding the 640 acres of our university property. As a direct result, business owners providing leadership to the economic development group adopted the Campus District concept as one of its primary sectors for further development.

In turn, this led to the initiation of a joint campus-community task force designed to create goals and objectives related to the development of the campus district. Representatives from both the Mansfield and Ontario city councils and mayoral offices populated this task force, alongside business owners serving as representatives of the economic development group, the county government commissioners, and senior members of our co-located institutions of higher learning. Some of the initial actions undertaken by this group included the provision of support during negotiations surrounding water and sewer issues, advocacy for such structural concerns as road modifications and sidewalk improvements, and writing grants in support of a study to better understand the residential needs and retail capacity of the area.

The impact of elected and appointed government officials

The contributions made by business and industry leaders in turn impacted the contributions of elected and appointed government officials. As noted above, the Campus District joint planning committee was comprised of representatives of two mayoral offices and several countywide departments, in addition to the regular complement of business owners. As a result, there simply was no way that the economic development plans for the area surrounding our campus were going to proceed without the explicit support of elected officials of the towns most affected by this initiative.

What is not as readily discerned here is the rather long history of mutual distrust and conflict between the local municipalities involved in the Campus District that had to be overcome in order to make this effort work.

Fortunately, mayors who were not personally involved in previous disputes came into office just before the Campus District initiative was launched. Also, a new county commissioner with a great deal of "can do spirit" was elected not long after. And while it certainly helped that this commissioner was widely seen by many as a rising star in government circles, even more impactful was the fact that she was a graduate of the local technical college that co-existed on our campus. Nothing speaks louder or with more clarity than an alumnus who can tell the story of how important a local institution of higher learning was to their own personal success.

It is also essential to note that the new commissioner was a former mayor herself, and therefore could not only "talk the talk" but also "walk the walk" when engaged in economic development discussions with the mayors of Mansfield and Ontario. As mayor, she also was the founder of what eventually become known as Leader Richland, a program designed to bring seventh and eighth graders from school districts throughout the county to our campus to spend a day engaged in experiential activities that fostered an understanding of the relationship between educational pursuits and career development. This initiative continues to expand, and presently includes students from 90% of the local school districts surrounding the Mansfield campus.

Further, the quiet but consequential backstage support for all of these economic development activities had been consistently provided by our local state representative, Mark Romanchuk, whose quote that "we are a college town, we just don't know it" was used at the beginning of the introductory remarks in this book. A local business owner as well as a state representative, Mark Romanchuk keenly understood the connection between education and economic development, and as such had become a tireless supporter of our town-gown efforts.

The impact of non-profit leaders

The local United Way was a natural partner for many faculty-led and student-involved projects that had town-gown relationship implications, including the service learning courses mentioned earlier. Here, both direct and indirect support came through grants that would fund projects that were connected to the service learning efforts emanating from our campus and implemented in the community. As well, the United Way leadership team helped to convene local non-profit agencies at those times when our campus needed to gather critical feedback from these stakeholders, including perhaps most importantly the implementation of focus groups both before and after our campus-community survey efforts on town-gown relationships (as discussed in Chapter 6). On a related note, the local United Way director also helped to solicit participation in the survey itself through the organization's email distribution lists.

The largest philanthropic organization in the area – the Richland County Foundation – also provided significant support for our town-gown efforts. This included direct grant support for our business and industry internship program, as well as convening stakeholders for various discussions on how the campus could improve its relationship with the community. Indirect support from this foundation also came in the way of their having supported further economic development activities beyond the actions taken by the Ohio State students, thus breathing continued life into the strategic planning efforts.

The impact of local school district leaders

The fact that our campus offered a teacher preparation program was a compelling enough reason to become more systematically engaged with representatives of local school districts. In addition, the largest school district in the immediate vicinity – Mansfield City Schools – was in dire need of help in terms of the academic performance of its students. Fortunately, several initiatives already had gained toeholds inside of this school district – including most notably the nationally recognized Algebra Project and Reading Recovery initiatives – by the time I had met their superintendent.

This individual was unlike any superintendent I had ever met before. He was willing to directly acknowledge student performance issues, he held his faculty members both in high regard and yet saw them as directly responsible for what was occurring in their classrooms, and he understood the need for more parental involvement in the educational process. After twenty-five plus years of banging my head against what I perceived to be the brick wall of the public educational system, I found someone who was prepared to open his district's doors to higher education, and sought more active involvement than our campus faculty members originally were prepared to offer.

We began our efforts to more fully engage each other by formulating a core question: What would happen if a school district, a university, and a community came together in support of local youth? A full year of planning discussions around that query led to our development of what became known as the "Beginning Anew" initiative, so named in order to connote the need for an initiative that blazed a new path of collaboration between public schools and universities.

And for the past three years, that is exactly what has been happening. In year one, we sought to make explicit the need for leaders in higher education, public schools, and the community to become co-responsible for the development and well-being of local youth. Building on this platform, in year two we examined the role that poverty played in impacting youth and family economic health. Against the backdrop of more recent incidents in Ferguson and Baltimore, year three's activities included an exploration of the impact that racial issues have had on individual, family, and community well-being.

Each year's events included both larger and smaller group discussions containing stakeholders representing both the town and gown sides of the equation, generated in meetings that were held both on campus and in the community. There is widespread anticipation regarding next year's focal point and planned activities. At this point, the Beginning Anew effort likely will center on bringing the topical areas of the last three years together under one umbrella in order to create an action plan that will spell out a more comprehensive P-16 approach (that is, preschool through college) to educating youth from Mansfield and other nearby school districts.

The impact of campus and community police forces

Our campus has enjoyed a very positive relationship among various law enforcement units. Mutual assistance agreements have been put in place among the local, county, and state patrol levels, for instance, and our campus has hosted a yearly breakfast gathering that brings law enforcement and public safety leaders together in a show of appreciation for all that they and their staff members do to keep our campus and communities safe.

The police chiefs of the local communities surrounding the campus also have been responsive to faculty and staff initiatives aimed at addressing a variety of quality of life issues. For instance, the Beginning Anew initiative discussed above included a town hall meeting on racial issues that included the very active involvement of the Mansfield police chief. More recently, both the Mansfield and Ontario police chiefs have met with the residential students of our campus at the beginning of the year as part of our welcoming events to discuss issues and concerns about student safety.

The impact of local media

The editor of the local paper and the general manager of the local television station historically have been strong supporters of the university. It helped that they (and many of their family members) were alumni of the university, of course. These and other media outlets have provided consistent, widespread, and positive coverage of campus activities over the years, including the ongoing work on the town-gown concerns discussed throughout this book. In addition to positioning campus events and updates as lead items wherever possible, our campus has enjoyed a variety of follow-up stories and articles that have placed us in a very favorable light in the eyes of the community. All of this would not be possible without a high level of professionalism on the part of media leadership, especially in terms of adhering to a longstanding desire to present newsworthy information in a fair and balanced manner.

The creation of an online news outlet in Richland County has served to further enhance our ability to communicate with our community stakeholders. In large part, the editor of this web-based information source has provided guidance and direction on the delivery of news that emphasizes the positive aspects of life in local communities, and has devoted ample attention to educational issues that have included the activities of our campus. Given the cutbacks that have taken place in the local newspaper and television staffs as a result of disruptions being experienced throughout the industry, the rise of this online newspaper has filled a void that otherwise might have significantly dampened our ability to get the word out on our successes.

Finally, the role that local radio stations have played in further developing clear channels of communication with community residents also has been significant. The opportunity to go on the air in both live and pre-recorded fashion through the process of being interviewed about campus updates and events has paid handsome dividends over the years, especially as the Campus District project was first being launched. Local radio personalities can and do have strong relationships with their listeners, and their interest in gaining the "inside story" about town-gown issues serves to create greater awareness and support among community residents.

The Quintessential Town-Gown President: E. Gordon Gee

The next section of this chapter is culled from a series of conversations I had with E. Gordon Gee who, at the time of this book's writing, had served as a university president at no less than five different major institutions of higher learning, including two different stints at The Ohio State University and West Virginia University. As part of a writing project that he and I were undertaking on town-gown relationships and the land grant mission, we spoke quite a bit about the impact that university presidents have on campus-community interaction. President Gee graciously agreed to allow me to include in this book some essential insights regarding the town-gown experiences he has accumulated over his thirty plus years in office.

The transcription of Dr. Gee's responses to each of my questions is provided in full. In turn, additional commentary about how these remarks fit within the intentional leadership issues that have been raised throughout this book in offered.

Describe the learning process you experienced regarding town-gown relationships across your seven stints as a university president.

"There is nothing more important than having a great relationship with your city. My belief is this. You can't have a great university and a shoddy city. And you can't have a great city without a great higher educational system. Therefore, it's incredibly important to work diligently to ensure that those town-gown relationships are powerful and positive. I've had experiences on both sides of that equation, experiences where those relationships were not as powerful and as positive as they could be, and others that were."

"The truth of the matter is — and I have come to this conclusion after 35 years — the university is about two things: talent and culture. And in order to create effective town-gown relationships, a president must bend and shape the university's talent and culture towards the needs and desires of the community."

Here we see the great wisdom that comes from three decades of experience as a university president. There is no question in President Gee's mind that the town-gown relationship is one of the most important agenda items for any college or university president. As he indicated in his remarks, there is no way that an institution of higher learning can achieve greatness without the surrounding communities also being of a sufficiently high quality. This sentiment was echoed repeatedly by the presidents interviewed for this book (as reported in chapter seven), and is also found within the quotes of presidents originally contained in the *Leadership in Higher Education* book written by Francis Lawrence.

At the same time, we must not lose sight of the parallel notion that the vast majority of towns and cities across our nation able to maintain a higher quality of life are those that contain colleges and universities. In this regard, one of the earliest quotes used in this book on this subject matter came from Mike Fox, who noted that municipalities *without* institutions of higher learning can only wish that they did, in fact, have a college or university in their midst. But this idea needs to be taken a step farther. Those towns and cities that are thriving places to live typically have *robust* colleges and universities within their municipal boundaries. Hence, it's not really enough for a town or city merely to have an institution of higher learning within its boundaries. To be a truly a great place to live, that college or university must be thriving.

President Gee ended this particular response by focusing on the bending and shaping of university talent and university culture in service to meeting the needs of the community. It's important to extend this line of thinking to note that all of the accumulated talent in the world will be for naught if there is no cultural context on campus that can support high quality town-gown relationships. Likewise, a community-friendly environment on campus that does not contain the personnel who are skilled in developing and maintaining mutually beneficial town-gown interactions quickly will become an exercise in futility for both sides. In the end, therefore, this is a both/and proposition: only talent and culture applied in combination will win the day.

When you were at The Ohio State University you formulated the "One University" concept: where did it come from conceptually?

"The one university concept came from my experiences as president of some smaller institutions. The fact is that they are unified, and they can speak with one voice. They can be very agile and very creative. And so when I returned to Ohio State, all of the sudden I realized that there were some very real impediments that were the result of our great size. We were a cacophony. We had multiple and differing interests in each of the colleges that made up the university. Those colleges each had their own agendas and infrastructures. Sometimes there was alignment, and other times they were in conflict with one another."

"Both in terms of cost and quality, I felt that it was necessary for us to start to unify within the institution so that we could become more a more powerful and positive force in the community. The power of The Ohio State University, and the power of West Virginia University for that matter, is their great size. But if size becomes an impediment instead of an asset, why have such an institution, I thought? So my goal was to have the physicians and philosophers lay down like lambs and lions. I had to bring these many and varied voices together."

Let us start here with the notion that size does in fact matter. We can imagine four very different configurations of town-gown relationships (see Table 2) as a function of relative mass: 1) the larger college/university that exists within a smaller town; 2) the larger college/university situated in a larger city; 3) the smaller college/university contained within a larger city; and 4) the smaller college/university that exists within the boundaries of a smaller town.

Table 2: Differential Size Combinations

Small College/University & Small Municipality	Small College/University & Large Municipality
Large College/University & Small Municipality	Large College/University & Large Municipality

President Gee notes that the great size of The Ohio State University's flagship campus, contained within the fifteenth largest city in the nation, presents certain challenges and opportunities inherent to the "big fish in a big pond" situation. Of course, West Virginia University also is a large university, but it exists within a much smaller municipality (Morgantown has slightly less than 30,000 permanent residents according to 2010 census figures). While there certainly are some overlapping features, West Virginia University has some very distinct challenges and opportunities as a "big fish in a small pond" when compared to Ohio State's situation. Still different are the issues and concerns faced by schools that are either "little fish in big ponds" or "little fish in little ponds," of course.

Much more work is needed to articulate the comparison and contrast of these challenges and opportunities as a function of campus and community size. Undoubtedly, the literature on town-gown relationships would be enriched by the further exploration of the different size combinations found in Table 2. Further, the examination of potential differences between public and private institutions also bears further scrutiny in light of these various configurations.

How does a university maintain town-gown relationships when they have multiple campuses that are geographically distinct?

"When I then thought about Ohio State's six campuses, my objective was to have each of them serve as front doors to the university, and not side doors. And the reason for that is I wanted people to have easy access to a great university, no matter where they lived in the state. This was the only way to fulfill the land grant mission of the university, and therefore to keep the promise that has been made to every

citizen of Ohio."

"To make this work, however, we had to have dynamic leaders placed at each of the campus locations. And those leaders had to be connected back to the Columbus campus. The only way you are going to get a unified voice in an institution as big as Ohio State is to have leaders who are focused on that unified approach, regardless of where the campus is located geographically."

At first glance, one might assume that the challenges of multiple campuses only exist within the larger public universities. After all, these are the institutions of higher learning that are well known for having statewide reach with their regional or branch campuses. However, even the smallest two-year technical and community colleges are confronted with issues and concerns surrounding the coordinated management of multiple campus sites as those institutions have sought to develop and maintain physical presences in the different communities they serve. In dealing with this issue, again we hear President Gee getting back to his main point about the need to bend and shape the talent and culture of the university. This time, however, his focus is more directly on the workings of the leadership team itself.

In order to make the most sense out of what Dr. Gee is suggesting here, I am going to employ a family science concept known as differentiation. Those families that are functioning best are those that are highly differentiated, which describes a family environment where its members experience both high connectivity with one another while simultaneously retaining the ability to function autonomously as needed. In contrast, less functional families are less differentiated, meaning that they experience lower levels of connectedness and/or lower levels of autonomy.

The college or university that contains multiple campuses also must display its own type of high differentiation among its leaders. They must all be on the same page in order to speak with a unified voice, for instance. That's part of the connectivity piece. And yet they also must be dynamic enough leaders to be able to independently respond to those special issues and concerns that arise as a function of the idiosyncratic nature of their individual campuses.

The business community seems to wield great influence in determining the nature of the town-gown relationship. What have you learned about working with business leaders?

"Business leaders have very strong views, they have very strong personal interests, and they usually have very strong economic interests. They must be at the table as partners with the university. As president, you can't be a fullback and run over these people. You can't be a bully, and you can't be arrogant. You have to listen carefully, but at the same time you have to be a strong advocate for the interests of the university. And if you build solid relationships with the business community on issues that are mutually beneficial, when conflict arises it doesn't escalate into all-

out war."

The focus on the business community is the first portion of a two part act (see the focus on politicians in the next section of this chapter) where you simply have to "follow the money" in order to understand how things work within more harmonious town-gown relationships. Readers will recall that there was great uniformity of opinion from the presidents and city managers interviewed for this book (as reported in chapter seven) regarding the critical influence of business owners on campus-community interaction. After all, these individuals have the greatest impact on the economic health of a community, creating and maintaining jobs for residents seeking workplace opportunities. In many cases, business and industry leaders also are the individuals most likely to contribute larger sums of money in the form of donations to both the needs of the campus and the philanthropic requirements of the community.

President Gee was quick to point out the need for respectful dialogue to take place between university and business leaders that will result in mutually beneficial town-gown activities. The idea of creating reciprocally advantageous outcomes for the campus and community is firmly lodged in the best practices literature reviewed earlier in this book. Phrases such as "lasting partnerships," "meaningful participation" and "common destiny" were used in the second chapter to describe the ways that institutions of higher learning and municipalities can join together to reach goals that lift both sides to greater heights.

What about the role that elected officials play in town-gown relationships, both locally and at the state and federal levels? What have you learned about working with politicians?

"I love working with elected officials. It's part of the sausage-making that creates a great university. With politicians especially, it's all about establishing personal relationships. It's important to get to know them and their families. Family relationships are terribly important in this business. I meet sons and daughters and wives and husbands and I give them calls once in a while, just to check up on them, to wish them happy birthdays and whatnot. And all of this is important because you don't want to treat politicians just as politicians. You want to treat them like they are part of your family."

"I believe that the one common ground that we all have politically is our university system. Colleges and universities are neither Republican nor Democrat. They are not red or blue. The Ohio State University is scarlet and gray. And that's our politics here, those are our political colors. And so I don't care what side of the aisle a politician is from. What I care about is making that politician care about the university and its values."

Here is the second act of the "follow the money" declaration made above in terms of more fully understanding how harmonious town-gown relationships work. In this latter case, the focus is on the interactions of university leaders and politicians. President Gee focused attention on the "sausage making" of government as a critical component of how great universities are built and maintained. It is axiomatic to state that public institutions have a large vested interest in developing positive interactions with legislators at the state level. After all, they are the representatives who oversee decision-making processes surrounding tuition and fees, state subsidy arrangements, and capital appropriations for new construction projects and the renovation and repair of existing buildings on campus.

Further, leaders of both public and private institutions share a common interest in developing strong affiliations with politicians at both the local and federal levels. In addition to influencing the various ways that federal dollars flow to students in the way of Pell grants and other forms of student aid, United States senators and representatives can provide funding for projects that would be of great immediate benefit to the economic well-being of campuses and communities across the nation. While thinking more globally, higher education officials more often must act locally, and that implies the need to work closely with elected officials of the municipalities surrounding their campuses. That's the most expedient way to get things done in your own backyard, after all.

President Gee's emphasis on understanding the more personal side of a given politician's life – in essence treating that individual as a part of one's own extended family – rings true here, especially in combination with the idea of transcending party affiliations. After all, members of a family can choose to be Democrats, Republicans, Independents, Tea Party enthusiasts, etc., and still come together when it comes to family loyalties and obligations. With enough perseverance, according to Dr. Gee, politicians on both sides of the aisle can come together in united support of the university.

What about the leaders of non-profit agencies, including such organizations as the United Way? What have you learned about working with these groups when it comes to building healthy town-gown relationships?

"This is another essential component of town-gown relations. If the university doesn't give to the community, how can we ask the community to support the university? We need to put a lot of emphasis on contributing to United Way and other programs. And when we are successful in doing that, then we can go to the community and say that we are full participants in the life of this community."

"One of the things that I have done at West Virginia University is to create something called the Million Hour Match. As a university, we have pledged to match one million hours of community service to the cities and counties in the state that provide their own programs to local citizens. Together, we will provide two million hours of community-building activities to the state of West Virginia."

If students are the "tip of the sword" when it comes to town-gown relationships, the pointy part of the blade often finds its mark in the community. Wielded haphazardly, the rapier creates a mess, as references to student misbehavior throughout this book would indicate. Properly sheathed, however, a sword becomes an attractive adornment instead of (or at least in addition to) being seen only as a potential weapon of destruction.

Without stretching this metaphor too far, the thrust of students into the community looks much shinier and prettier when they are doing positive things for the citizenry. Partnerships with the local non-profit organizations would seem to be one of the more efficient means by which institutions of higher learning can make these good works happen in a very visible manner. The presidents and city managers interviewed for this book certainly corroborated this point through the many references they made to the powerful positive message that is transmitted when students are seen as working for the betterment of the community.

Many presidents are implored to foster significant contact between their campuses and local schools, especially around issues concerning education quality. What have you learned about working with K-12 leaders over the years?

"The bedrock of our democracy is the public school system. And the bedrock of great universities is built on those schools sending us great students. And yet all too often the universities get turned into educational Red Cross units, to correct the ills

of public schools. Now of course we can't be an extension of every public school in the state. But we can put on principal academies, for instance. And we can set high standards for admission to the university, which the raises the bar for public school performance. At the end of the day, you would be foolish not to be fully engaged with the schools as a university leader because we have to have bright students sent to us."

Here we find President Gee rather candidly noting the significant self-interest that colleges and universities have in helping to raise the quality of educational activities taking place in the public school systems in their student recruitment zones. Most simply put, these are the feeder systems for students who potentially will matriculate into a given institution of higher learning. Provide help that raises the quality bar, he argues, and eventually you raise the academic readiness levels of students who will be applying for admission.

At the same time, however, Dr. Gee cautions university leaders about getting involved at a crisis intervention level within the local schools. This point was echoed within several sets of remarks made by the presidents interviewed for this book. There is only so much attention that can be given to any single school or school district before resource allocation becomes a significant issue. Involvement in the schools therefore becomes a sort of balancing act for colleges and universities: not too little – especially if you have a teacher preparation program within your institution – and not too much.

When it comes to the senior management teams you have worked with across your presidencies, how have you most effectively created alignment on town-gown issues?

"First of all, getting any kind of alignment with your senior leadership teams is one of the most difficult challenges facing university presidents. Very often it's hand to hand combat. People who reach that level have tremendously strong views and egos. And so you have to start with senior leadership in order to introduce the kind of cultural transformation that will allow a university to become fully engaged with the community. They have to set the tone regarding the importance of town-gown relationships."

"Saying that, you must understand that every institution is different. When I was younger I used to think of these things as fungible commodities. And they're not. They're very distinct. Realizing that, you need to make sure that you get a really clear understanding of the culture, and then tailor your team-building efforts into that culture. And then you have to find the right point person to lead the town-gown effort within your senior staff."

Within the interviews conducted with presidents and city administrators for this book, there was some interesting variation regarding opinions expressed about how university leaders can best assign responsibilities related to town-gown efforts. On the one hand, there was some support for a more centralized process whereby one individual – preferably high ranking enough to have significant decision-making authority – was put in charge of campus-community activities. In contrast, other opinions were shared that distributed those responsibilities among several senior administrators according to their position descriptions.

President Gee is agnostic about this issue. In fact, he asserts that senior staffs are not unlike snowflakes; that is, from a distance they all look alike, but up close you see interesting variations at the individual level. Savvy university leaders will recognize the tendencies of the culture they have inherited, and then adapt their ideas and activities to best suit that environment.

Those same perceptive leaders also will recognize what works best for their community partners. In some situations, it may be the case that nothing less than the president's consistent physical presence in joint planning meetings will generate meaningful and authentic relationships with some municipal leaders. In other cases, what may be more important is the simple knowledge that the president can be contacted directly by a city administrator should the need arise. As reported in chapter seven, at least one town manager pointed directly to the power of having the university president's personal cell phone number on speed dial.

What has worked best in terms of encouraging faculty member involvement in the community, and how have you viewed "counting" this town-gown work in promotion and tenure decisions?

"Within public universities, you have certain areas of the faculty such as in medicine that are fully engaged in the community because they are providing health care services for patients. Agriculture also is fully engaged through extension services, because that's their calling. But other parts of the university tend to be much more isolated, and it's because of the type of work that they do. They're almost likes monks in a cave, if you know what I mean.

"I think what you don't do is try to force everyone into getting engaged. Instead, you find champions – I'm a great believer in champions – and in a large public university you have natural champions and let them run with it. You can find those champions in education and the arts as well. They are community minded, and you ask them to become part of a change process as champions."

"However, until you totally renovate the reward and recognition process for faculty, you're not going to get to where you need to. Until we get rid of the McDonald's hamburger approach to recognizing and rewarding faculty, you're going to be putting new wine into old bottles with your town-gown approach. Even though we say that faculty are supposed to be teaching, conducting research, and engaging in service, right now we know that the coin of the realm is research. And for those that are going to do cutting edge research, that's wonderful. But we need to recognize that some people are excellent teachers, and others care about community engagement,

201

and we should let them do that without creating the sense that they are second-class citizens."

There are a lot of issues contained in this last extended quote that deserve to be unpacked. First, it is absolutely true that some disciplines lend themselves more readily to engagement in the community. Medical schools and nursing colleges need patients in order to teach health care delivery, for instance, and agricultural schools have a strong historical tie to communities through their extension programs. This is not to say that humanities scholars cannot engage citizens, of course, but the very nature of their work makes it less likely that these faculty members would benefit as immediately and directly from such contact.

Dr. Gee's preference for outreach and engagement "champions" to emerge and carry out such work has great merit. However, he rightfully notes that, until the university reward system undergoes a rather radical modification, community-based efforts typically will be given short shrift, especially in more research intensive institutions. There appears to be some interesting variation among the presidents interviewed for this book regarding their having actively thought about changes to the promotion and tenure system. Those presidents who placed greater emphasis on community engagement as part of their personal stamp on town-gown relationships were those individuals who reported more intensive attempts to foster dialogue about the need to change the reward system.

That said, it must be remembered that the presidents interviewed for this book all came out of large research-based institutions of higher learning. It is fair to expect that a very different set of expectations and reward structures might be found in interviews with presidents of smaller colleges and universities. And as mentioned before, there also are potential differences that might be found when the public versus private institution distinction is applied.

Those of us who know you well are familiar with your extraordinary emphasis on being involved directly in the lives of students. How has that been translated into your views on building more harmonious town-gown relationships?

"At the end of the day, university presidents are relatively unimportant people within the university. But their efforts to set the tone and values of the place are the most important things that presidents do. And therefore it's important that students see a president that is excited about them and is excited about their engagement in the community. That is my calling, and my responsibility."

"People have talked about working hard and playing hard as a student. I want to talk about working smart and playing smart. And the smart part is that we want to recognize our students as adults, and give them the immense responsibility of refining their own culture, rather than treating them as kids. And once we do that, then we are going to reach that equilibrium point where we see effective student

engagement in the community."

This may be one of the more astonishing insights offered by President Gee. Throughout the transcribed interviews of presidents conducted for this book, there is some sense of a *parens patriae* doctrine at work in their thinking about the student body of their institutions. That is, the presidents often alluded to the need to protect or otherwise limit students from engaging in self-destructive behaviors, which sometimes carried the additional consequence of creating harm to the community. And nowhere was this more clearly stated than in the realm of alcohol consumption.

Instead, Dr. Gee offers the viewpoint that we recognize and treat college students as *adults*. While some readers might say that this is easier said than done, and immediately reject this stance as unrealistic, it might be wise to ponder such a viewpoint for at least a couple of moments longer. After all, this line of thinking does connect with the sentiments of at least one of the university presidents interviewed for this book, who had offered up the lament that greater attention might have been paid to the civic education of students during his tenure.

Another area of scholarship that can shed some additional light here is the body of work done on labeling theory. This is a set of theoretical premises that assumes people act in accordance with the labels (and accompanying expectations) that others assign to them. Often employed by criminologists, labeling theory in essence asserts that a self-fulfilling prophecy occurs among people who are described as "bad" or "delinquent." It should not be too difficult to imagine that undergraduate students might also be acting in stereotypical ways – getting drunk, smoking pot, rioting in the streets after athletic events, etc. – precisely because they are expected to behave in that manner.

That said, readers do not have to wholeheartedly buy into the all of the premises of labeling theory to see some potential value in shifting student attention away from the work hard/play hard mentality and toward the work smart/play smart distinction made by President Gee. And nowhere might this be more fruitful than in the area of community outreach and engagement. If a college or university begins to expect (or perhaps even require) that its students become more involved in the community, it is infinitely more likely to actually happen.

A president is answerable to the governing board. What have you learned over the years about board of trustees members and town-gown issues?

"Different boards respond in different ways, and board members all have their own personal points of view about the importance of town-gown relationships. It's not always easy to manage a board into thinking that this is incredibly important. At Ohio State for instance I had board members that thought this was incredible nonsense, and that we should be investing in medicine or education or something

205

else. So you have to be tenacious in pursuit of what you are doing, and constantly communicating with them. At the same time, you must remember that your time will come to leave, or get fired, because your friends come and go but your enemies accumulate. When you are assertive with your board, eventually the tipping point comes. I know this point very well."

Unfortunately, the interviews with university presidents did not contain any specific references to their work with the controlling boards they were answerable to during their tenure. Had that been the case, it would have been interesting to see how much their own personal experiences with board members matched up to President Gee's reflections.

That said, there were several informal mentions of interactions between governing board members and presidents scattered throughout these interviews. In some cases, the presidents were literally rolling their eyeballs as they described the negative reactions of board members to initiatives that the presidents wanted to undertake with and for the community. In other cases, the presidents reported more supportive reactions that coincided with board members actually joining in on the community engagement activity being described.

Of course, a president ultimately cannot go rogue – or at least cannot do so for too long or stray too far off the mark – without risking the loss of support from his or her board members. And that lack of support inevitably leads to removal. Therefore, it seems clear that one area that is ripe for further work surrounds the need to educate governing board members on the importance of town-gown relationships.

What advice would you give to newly installed university presidents regarding town-gown relationships?

"Move quickly. Don't spend a lot of time doing the typical listening tour. Don't spend a lot of time ruminating. I think that too many university presidents spend too much time being obscure. It's important that you get your sleeves rolled up and make a statement that town-gown relationships are very important to you. Engage with community leaders and find out what their problems and issues are, and how you can best engage with them to create solutions. Most university presidents spend most of their time inside, and they create an imbalance. You have to live cheek to jowl with the community."

These closing remarks find President Gee in great accord with the presidents interviewed for this book. To a person, each president would tell his less experienced self to immerse themselves fully in dialogue with community members in order to more fully understand their needs and desires. Once identified, Dr. Gee goes on to say, university presidents must then work directly with those community members to create solutions and effect change.

Summary

The main objective of this chapter was to highlight the need for "intentional leadership" within town-gown relationships. The story was told of how one campus and community went from being among the worst of relationship types – the devitalized town-gown relationship that is characterized by low effort and low comfort levels – to a much more healthy and functional pattern of interacting partners that care for one another's well-being, largely through the deliberate and collaborative efforts of university and municipal leaders. In turn, the contents of an interview conducted with E. Gordon Gee were included in order to underscore the critical impact that university presidents have on town-gown relationships, largely by shaping the talents and cultural of the people who together comprise the campus-community partnership.

9. THE TEN COMMANDMENTS OF TOWN-GOWN RELATIONSHIPS

The main objective of this ninth and final chapter of the book is to create closure for this body of work by providing some guidelines that campus and community leaders can use to build more harmonious town-gown relationships with one another. The statements that come next represent a first attempt to develop a set of "emerging best practices" for university and municipal leaders, generated as a result of combining the contents of this book with a thorough review of the town-gown literature.

Because there are exactly ten such statements, and to keep things a bit entertaining (perhaps resulting in a sort of pneumonic device as well), they will be referred to as the Ten Commandments of Town-Gown Relationships. With the further accumulation of future qualitative and quantitative data on this subject matter, scholars undoubtedly will wish to edit and refine this initial list. Hence, readers should consider these town-gown commandments to be scribbled in moist clay, rather than chiseled onto stone tablets.

Town-Gown Commandment #1: Thou shall give high priority to efforts that build more harmonious relationships between campus and community members.

It's a pretty good bet that readers who have made it to the last chapter of this book already have bought into the notion that town-gown relationships are important. This first commandment goes a step beyond mere recognition of the significant impact that campus and community partners can have on one another, however. Rather, it is an insistence that university and municipal leaders elevate the prioritization that they give to the accomplishment of those tasks that will improve their interaction with one another.

Of course, there are a lot of demands that compete for the attention of college and university presidents and city administrators. And nothing can refocus attention faster than an acute crisis, especially if that emerging predicament carries with it certain financial and/or human capital costs. Of course, the exact worst time to try building positive relationships is in the midst of dealing with a calamity. If the first commandment is followed, then campus and community leaders already will have made significant investments in town-gown relationships that are much more likely to weather the stressors and strains of a newly arising crisis event.

All of the university presidents and city administrators who were interviewed for this book were unanimous in their insistence that town-gown relationships remain front and center in the everyday thoughts and routine actions of campus and community leaders. If campus and community leaders are working together during periods of calm, the thinking goes, they are much more likely to withstand the headwinds of the next predicament they will face. These days, all too often it is a question of when, and not if, the next crisis will happen for university and municipal leaders.

Of course, the individuals interviewed for this book all were associated with thriving institutions and municipalities. Is that coincidental, or rather was this level of success due to their focus on town-gown relationships as an everyday matter? The latter case is quite likely, especially if one places stock in President Gee's statement in chapter eight that "you can't have a great university and a shoddy city. And you can't have a great city without a great higher educational system." Again and again, we heard from leaders who recounted the actions they undertook to intentionally build solid personal relationships with their counterparts on a regular basis, rather than interacting only around problems and difficulties.

There certainly has been more general support for this position within the land grant tradition of universities. The Morrill Act specifically called for universities to become regionalized partners with the communities that surrounded them, creating institutions of higher learning that would both shape and be shaped by local needs. As well, reinvigorated attention paid to the land grant mission over the last two decades led to the Kellogg Commission's admonition that universities assign greater important to campus-community partnerships on the way to becoming more "engaged institutions," as we discussed in the third chapter.

Also noted in that same chapter was the fact that other professional organizations created similar platforms by which to highlight the importance of campus-community interaction. This included the Carnegie Foundation's classification for community engagement, the focus on regional stewardship offered by the American Association of State Colleges and Universities, and the conceptualization of anchor institutions in communities as promoted by the Coalition of Urban and Metropolitan Universities. Taken together, it would seem as if the first commandment is universal in orientation, if not in actual practice.

Town-Gown Commandment #2: Thou shall not miscalculate the time involved in developing and maintaining harmonious campus-community relationships.

As we know from chapters three and four, the most desirable town-gown relationship is the harmonious type, which consists of both higher effort levels and higher comfort levels. When we examine marriages, we see that harmonious relationships exist when spouses report elevated satisfaction levels with one another (i.e. high comfort) in the midst of engaging in a lot of shared activities with one another (i.e. high effort). Similarly, we know that harmonious town-gown relationships are created when campus and community partners are successful in working together comfortably and continuously across a wide range of activities.

This second commandment recognizes that it takes a great deal of time and effort to maintain the harmonious relationship. Whether you are involved in a marriage or a town-gown partnership, you will find yourself in a high quality relationship only for as long as you are willing to do what it takes to maintain the relatively high levels of both effort and comfort. Said a little differently, if you want to be involved in a harmonious relationship, you are going to have to work for it.

Of course, all relationships take time to grow and develop. Harmonious relationships, however, take a great deal of time to promote, preserve, and protect. University presidents and city managers are extremely busy people, of course. And yet not one single individual interviewed for this book made the suggestion that a campus or community leader should reduce the amount of time they spend on town-gown relationships. Quite the opposite. As just one example, recall the one former university president who stated that "I might have devoted – even though I didn't have any more time, I was already doing hundred hour weeks – I could have squeezed out a little more time, spent a little more time with community leaders who were inclined to have a more suspicious view of the university and warm up to them." This is the viewpoint of someone who clearly has learned that the continuous investment of time in town-gown relationships will pay rich dividends over the long haul.

Town-Gown Commandment #3: Thou shall honor your campus and community partners.

Most simply put, do not take your relationship partners for granted, and treat them fairly at all times. This is as true of town-gown relationships as it is of marriage or any other important interpersonal relationship you are trying to maintain at a relatively high quality level. This third commandment might best be translated into the statement that partners must attempt to establish some sense of relative equality in the relationship if they are to thrive together within its confines.

The different size combinations of campuses and communities

discussed in chapter 8 may sometimes get in the way of fulfilling this directive, however. All too often, it seems to be the case that the university is the "bigger" partner; that is, the one with more resources and relative power. And with that greater leverage comes the temptation for leaders of institutions of higher learning to act unilaterally. After all, if I hold all the cards, the thinking might go, why shouldn't things go my way?

Recall from the third chapter all of the common mistakes that universities make to aggravate these sorts of situations. This includes the routine failure to include municipal partners in planning for changes the university would like to make, especially those alterations that inevitably will impact some portion of the community in a direct manner. It was argued that these types of relationship blunders generate a whole host of problems for campus and community leaders alike, and often as not lead to deterioration in the overall quality of the town-gown relationship.

In fact, these were the very reasons given in chapter four as to why universities and municipalities struggled to experience harmonious relationships with one another. The lack of integrated planning efforts left campus and community partners without the connective tissue that would have allowed them to form more harmonious relationships.

What is the antidote to this? Recall the one former university president interviewed for this book who noted that "I think the main thing from the university's standpoint is to be respectful. It's easy I think for the president of a very large university with a multibillion dollar budget to try to look down their nose at the local small town community mayor or town council." This individual went on to emphasize the importance he attached to including his community-based colleagues in a consistent and respectful dialogue as often as he could. Clearly, inequalities in budget size and other resources do not have to translate automatically into an unequal set of voices. Rather, it is a decision that is made within the dynamics of each and every unique town-gown relationship.

Of course, keeping this third commandment is not a one-sided affair, one where only colleges and universities are to blame if the town-gown relationship does not manifest itself in a harmonious form. Municipal leaders share responsibility for what occurs within campus-community interactions. Recall Michael Fox's best practices statements regarding community liaison and civic engagement work, with his special emphasis on the significant role that police and other public safety personnel can and do play in developing more harmonious town-gown relationships. Choices are made by police and other public safety officials – all of whom take their cues (if not direct orders) from elected city officials – to either adopt a "heavy hand" with students, for example, or instead to implement a more non-confrontation community policing orientation in matters concerning misbehavior. In a separate yet related realm, parking and zoning issues as handled by city administrators and council members also can and do play a significant role in setting the tone within the town-gown relationship.

Therefore, respect is always a two-way street, and so too is the responsibility for keeping the third town-gown commandment. Campus and community partners must strive to level the playing field wherever and whenever possible. When relationship partners find themselves in the "one up" position, they should work diligently to make sure the wishes of their colleagues are heard and acknowledged before acting on the situation in question. And when relationship partners experience themselves as being in a "one down" position, they need to speak up – respectfully, of course – in the hopes that their counterparts are ready and willing to hear their voices.

Town-Gown Commandment #4: Thou shall seek win-win outcomes wherever and whenever possible in campus-community interactions.

The description of harmonious relationship characteristics contained in chapter four included a discussion about the need for partners to act according to a "fair give and take" principle. That is, optimal town-gown relationship partners must strive to balance the achievement of individual goals and objectives with an involvement in those activities that are mutually beneficial to both campus and community. Hence, the fourth commandment underscores the idea that, wherever and whenever possible, decisions are made by town-gown partners that create mutual advantage for both university and municipal stakeholders.

The directive to seek reciprocally beneficial outcomes is consistent with the town-gown best practices literature reviewed in chapter three. For example, Sungri-Eryilmaz specifically highlighted the need to identify goals that are shared by campus and community partners alongside the stipulation that those collaborators respect and support each other's individual interests. Similarly, Porter and Grogan called for campus and community leaders to create economic development strategies that are designed to be mutually beneficial and sustainable over the long-term.

In turn, professional organizations have developed guidelines for their higher education members to follow that also resemble the "fair give and take" mantra. For example, the American Association of State Colleges and Universities (AASCU) has implored its members to become regional stewards, as much for reasons of economic and political survival as for the enhancement of the student experience. AASCU, it was highlighted in chapter three, has argued that those member institutions that are vitally connected to the health and well-being of their local communities will be more likely to enjoy the support of the general public and, therefore, will be more likely to generate reliable sources of revenue over the long haul.

By all accounts, the most tried and true strategy for developing and maintaining mutually beneficial goals and objectives is the formation of a joint campus-community planning committee. One significant piece of evidence supporting this assertion is the description of the Joint City/University Advisory Board found in in chapter four, which was named by Jeff Martin as the single biggest factor that contributed to the harmonious relationship developed between Clemson University and the City of Clemson. This town-gown planning committee – comprised of equal numbers of city and university employees, and co-led by city council, the community police force, and the university president's council – was instrumental in both jumpstarting the creation of mutually beneficial objectives for the campus and community, as well as in generating the means by which these objectives were met over time.

Many of the former university presidents and city administrators interviewed for this book also credited their experiences with joint planning committees as having promoted more optimal town-gown interactions. Again and again, these individuals told us that the path toward a more harmonious relationship was founded on the hard work of hammering out mutually beneficial solutions to challenges and concerns in those meetings that included both campus and community leaders.

For instance, recall the one city manager who said that "it wasn't just show and tell, we got at economic development, and housing, and police and community relations. The tough issues. And we kept at them with the expectation that, in three months, there was going to be progress made on these issues." Other individuals interviewed for this book also acknowledged the powerful impact that joint planning committees have had on the quality of the town-gown relationship they inherited. One former university president, in noting that there was a town-gown committee already in place by the time he had arrived, stated that this "committee was the formalization of what had already been a very positive relationship between the university and the community."

In some very real ways, the first four commandments all build on one another. The first commandment insists that campus and community leaders have to make town-gown relationships one of their highest priorities. The second commandment demands that these leaders must dedicate a significant amount of their time to the development and maintenance of these prioritized relationships. It's not a priority if you aren't expending effort, after all.

In turn, the third commandment requires that the playing field must be kept as level as possible between the campus and community partners through their active and ongoing attempts to build and sustain reciprocal respect. Otherwise, one or both of the partners will downgrade the town-gown relationship in favor of other pursuits that generate more favorable returns on the investment of their time and energy. All of this brings us to the fourth commandment, which ties the first three directives together by asserting the proviso that the best goals and objectives for campus and community partners are those that create mutually beneficial outcomes.

Town-Gown Commandment #5: Thou shall remember that students are the most important point of connection between campus and community.

Embedded in the quantitative data gathered with the Optimal College Town Assessment (OCTA) tool to date, and inherent in many of the quotes taken from the interviews of campus and community leaders, is the idea that students – for better and for worse – are at the very heart of all town-gown relationships. Of course, students are the very reason that universities exist. They are sent by their families from communities that support the notion that higher education is a path toward great success in life. Some students will return to those very same communities once their college education is complete, while others will live in new communities. Regardless, they will take their place as part of the fabric of adult life in those communities, and they will be ever more successful in doing so if they have learned how to function as a productive community member.

As part of the information on best practices that was reviewed in chapter three, the work of Bruning and colleagues was highlighted as having described student-oriented activities that led to strengthened campus-community ties. More specifically, these scholars wrote about how town-gown relationships were fostered through any number of student experiences on campus and in the community. This included, but was not limited to, student access to community-based resources through such vehicles as internships, service learning opportunities, and volunteer activities.

These sorts of student activities also were mentioned repeatedly as a force for good in many of the comments made throughout the interviews conducted for this book. There was one city administrator who clearly admired the various ways his university president had challenged students to become "university stewards" for the communities in which they lived. That individual went on to note that this president "said that there are folks in your life that help you get to where you want to go in your life, and because of that you have a responsibility to give back. And he really pushed student service in the community and volunteering at non-profit agencies."

This underscores the commonsense notion that the Optimal College Town Assessment dimensions of effort and comfort are significantly and positively related to one another. To wit, the more effort that is expended by campus and community members, the greater the comfort levels that are generated within the town-gown relationship. This seems to be particularly true of efforts undertaken by students, whose efforts seem to "count" more than those of other campus representatives.

The account I gave of my own campus-community relationship renaissance provided some compelling evidence in support of this notion. Recall I had noted that there was significant student involvement in a number of activities, including well-known community philanthropic projects, service as campus ambassadors during campus outreach and engagement initiatives in the community, and participation in the development of a countywide economic development plan. Taken together, these types of student-oriented experiences were thought to have played a critical role in moving the campus and community toward a more harmonious relationship over time.

Of course, student activities that take on a more negative tone also seem to be weighted more heavily by community stakeholders. This fact led many of the former presidents and city managers to recognize the extremely complex nature of community perceptions of college students. In the words of one city administrator interviewed for this book: "It's so complex, and it changes daily. All that needs to happen is one bad incident with students, and the relationship can change a hundred and eighty degrees."

The power of student misbehavior was a significant component of the types of regrets expressed by the former presidents toward the end of each of their interviews. These presidents greatly sympathized with the plight of community members who were exposed to students getting out of hand in residential neighborhoods, stating that they certainly wouldn't want those sorts of activities occurring near their own homes. And to a person, each president laid the blame directly on alcohol overconsumption.

At the same time, at least one president suggested that the solution to these displays of antisocial behavior involved a civics education process that would instill the sense that students had significant responsibilities to the community within which they were getting their educations. He went on to discuss this as "a civil consciousness, a recognition that they are living in a community and that they have obligations even though they are only temporary residents."

This lines up rather nicely with the recommendation made by President Gee in chapter eight that students work smart and play smart. He went on to say that "the smart part is that we want to recognize our students as adults, and give them the immense responsibility of refining their own culture, rather than treating them as kids. And once we do that, then we are going to reach that equilibrium point where we see effective student engagement in the community." Therefore, this fifth commandment can be seen as hinging on the notion that students will maximally and positively impact town-gown relationships when they are incorporated into the community with more adult like status and responsibilities.

Town-Gown Commandment #6: Thou shall know the power of your alumni, especially those living in communities immediately surrounding the campus.

All community members matter, of course, and all students matter when it comes to making town-gown relationships what they are. Those students who, upon graduation, decide to remain as longer-term residents of the community then must *really* matter. In fact, the alumni who live in close proximity to a campus can and should have a special place in one's thinking about town-gown relationships. They are the perfect blend of campus and community. And for that reason, both university administrators and city managers alike should seek to nurture relationships with alumni living in those communities that surround the college or university from which they have graduated.

In the case example describing The Ohio State University at Mansfield campus, countless illustrations were provided of alumni making significant contributions to the well-being of the campus and community. The company that built the off-campus student housing was owned and operated by alumni who wanted to make a substantial impact on the growth potential of the regional campus, for example. Alumni serving as advisory board members were some of the most formidable advocates for strengthening town-gown relationship ties along economic development lines. The local alumni organizations played a critical role in generating annual support for scholarships through various fundraising activities. And so on.

As noted in chapter seven, there were several university presidents interviewed by Francis Lawrence in the 2006 book *Leadership in Higher Education* who highlighted the essential role that alumni played in the development and maintenance of higher quality town-gown relationships. Recall for example the words of Brit Kirwan, who admitted to not really understanding the importance of campus-community linkages when he first took office. Through a sustained focus on a number of external relations fronts, however, including specific efforts to reinvigorate the alumni operations office, he experienced great success in this area.

Another example from this same book was provided by David Ward in his discussion of the vital connection between higher education and the business community. He noted that "I tended to work through the UW alumni association and the UW foundation to reach the business community in order to focus on people who already had some connection and loyalty to Madison." Alumni who became business leaders in the local community also received particular attention from President Gee in the remarks he made in chapter eight. He saw them as an amalgamation of alumni, employers, and donors who "wore multiple hats" as advocates for both the university and the communities in which they resided.

Town-Gown Commandment #7: Thou shall respect the notion that faculty members represent the face of both campus and community.

Faculty members normally and typically are thought of in terms of making town-gown contributions from the campus side of things, of course. They are responsible for leading the service learning courses that many students use as their entry point into community engagement, for example. As well, they often as not are actively involved in the community through their own scholarship and service activities. This is especially true of medical faculty, who provide health care services to residents, and those science and engineering faculty members who contribute empirical assistance to various business and industry sponsors in the way of research and development activities. Faculty members in the social and behavioral sciences whose scholarship is more applied in orientation (i.e. translational research) also more frequently are involved in the community in order to gather data for their empirically-based activities.

Scholarship activities aside, however, some faculty members also are residents of the neighborhoods and communities immediately surrounding the campuses on which they are employed. Some of the university presidents and city administrators interviewed for this book recognized the dual role that is played by these faculty members. Referring to these faculty members who resided close to campus as "ambassadors to the city," one city administrator noted that they "had a great credibility, they had skin in the game, a lot at stake, and they were highly regarded. And we would go to them, because we knew they had a voice on campus."

Situations that arise in connection with those faculty members who reside in close geographic proximity to the campus does not always translate into champagne and roses, however. Recall the one city manager who stated that "some of the most difficult relationships have been between faculty members acting as residents in their relationship with the university versus their employment role." Therefore, to keep the seventh town-gown commandment, it is best to assume that faculty members who also are actively engaged in the community as local residents create complex sets of issues that are not easily categorized as good or bad. In fact, sometimes these resident faculty members can and do make both positive and negative contributions to certain situations at the same time.

Beyond the commandment itself, it should be emphasized that faculty members historically have struggled to have their work in the community recognized as making a valuable contribution within the university environment itself. Dr. Gee indicated in chapter eight that, as long as research is the coin of the realm in academia, outreach and engagement activities will be perceived as a less important activity. The former presidents that were interviewed for this book similarly echoed an awareness of the dynamic tension that existed between scholarship and service, at least insomuch as what is most highly prized and rewarded.

There are individuals and organizations presently seeking to change this dynamic, however. One excellent example here is the Engagement Scholarship Consortium (engagementscholarship.org), a membership-based entity consisting of universities whose stated goal is to "work collaboratively to build strong university-community partnerships anchored in the rigor of scholarship, and designed to help build community capacity." Originally founded by a number of larger land grant universities (Penn State, Ohio State, and Wisconsin were three of its earliest members), this Consortium has grown to over thirty institutional members. Organizational activities include the hosting of an annual meeting, as well as sponsoring several events throughout a given year that are designed to build and maintain networks of professionals involved in engagement scholarship.

In addition, two journals – the *Journal of Community Engagement and Scholarship* and the *Journal of Higher Education Outreach and Engagement* – are supported by the Engagement Scholarship Consortium for faculty members who are interested in publishing their work in this area. Recall the words of one university president who lamented that "I don't know if I can be sympathetic to those who say that I've done all of this service, but I don't have any research." Translation: if you aren't writing about it, it doesn't count. Hence, these publication outlets go a long way toward combatting the perception that faculty members are "just" engaged in service, at least for those individuals who are willing to document their community involvement through such scholarship efforts.

Town-Gown Commandment #8: Thou shall appreciate the history of the campus-community relationship you inherited.

If you are about to accept a new senior administration role on a campus or within a community, you may be lucky enough to inherit a harmonious town-gown relationship. Not so fortunate, in contrast, are those individuals who are about to walk into situations where the effort and comfort levels are, shall we say, less than ideal. Either way, knowing what you are getting yourself into in terms of previous patterns of campus-community interaction is an extremely important reconnaissance matter.

Without an awareness of the ebb and flow of the town-gown relationship from a historical perspective, campus and community leaders will not receive the benefit of lessons learned by their predecessors. Knowing what has worked – and perhaps even more importantly what has not worked – is an essential component of any town-gown relationship.

There is a certain fluidity to these town-gown relationships, of course. Harmonious relationships can deteriorate over time if not managed well, for instance, and even the most longstanding devitalized relationships can be rebuilt into something much more mutually satisfying for campus and community partners. And as we learned from the interviews conducted with university presidents and city managers, events surrounding student behavior (especially *mis*behavior) can turn a town-gown relationship on a dime.

That said, few if any relationships are truly all positive or all negative in orientation. This is as true of campus-community interaction as it is of a marriage. The trick then, if this can be boiled down to a single thought, is to adequately assess what has been "counted" – especially in terms of making contributions and creating difficulties – by the campus and community partners who have been dealing with one another over time.

An early family therapist by the name of Ivan Boszomenyi-Nagy proposed that all families keep a "family ledger," one that helps to determine what members both can expect to receive from their family and what they owe to their family based on their relative contributions over time (Boszormenyi-Nagy & Spark, 1973). It would seem fitting that this metaphor could be borrowed for present purposes in order to similarly examine the debits and credits that have been placed within the "town-gown ledger" by campus and community partners.

The identification of "debits" in the town-gown ledger most likely would come from conflicted and/or devitalized relationship histories, of course. As a result, there is almost a "therapeutic" component to the monitoring of this sort of information about campus-community interactions. After all, the first step in problem-solving is identifying the main issue at hand. Once you name it, you can deal with it.

Howard Zehr's (2002) work on restorative justice principles also can be borrowed here in terms of taking actions to call specific attention to past troubles between a given campus and community. In essence, leaders who adopt this type of strategy are seeking to place themselves in the position of "healing the harm" that often impedes working partnerships between campuses and communities. For example, apologizing for the mistakes made by one's predecessors can be a relatively low-cost and yet extraordinarily meaningful gesture that significantly increases the chances of improving situations where some historical offense had resulted in dramatically decreased comfort levels.

At the same time, it is just as important to identify the "credits" that have accumulated in the town-gown ledger. Acknowledging the positive contributions that individuals previously have made can and does allow campus and community partners to give praise where praise is due. A part of this strategy is to catch people "doing something right" whenever possible, even when those actions are historical in nature. On a related note, it's also about becoming more strength-based in your perception of town-gown relationships. As the saying goes, you either take the time to celebrate your successes, or pretty soon you won't have any successes to celebrate.

Town-Gown Commandment #9: Thou shall continuously assess the present state of the relationship between campus and community representatives.

The entire fifth chapter of this book was devoted to helping readers take the guesswork out of understanding the quality of their *present* town-gown relationships. Because there has been so little empirical work in this area, the focus of this chapter was centered on the development of a standardized measurement tool known as the Optimal College Town Assessment (OCTA). Two versions of the original 16 OCTA items were included in chapter five – one for campus representatives and the other for community stakeholders – in order to encourage readers to begin assessing their own town-gown relationships in a standardized manner.

The development of the OCTA was meant to be an antidote for the use of anecdote. That is, all too often campus and community partners regrettably have relied on anecdotal evidence when it comes to assessing and reporting on town-gown relationships. It's important to remember that adding two anecdotes together does not make data! And relying on circumstantial information gathered from a few conveniently located individuals on a campus or in a community is not only untrustworthy, it can be downright misleading and hence an ongoing threat to the integrity of town-gown relationships over time.

Some of the quantitative results generated in the initial pilot study using the OCTA items also were reported in chapter five. This included evidence surrounding some interesting variation in the effort and comfort levels reported by community stakeholders as a function of their physical distance from campus. Such findings should provide readers with a reason to ponder how geography may be playing a role in the quality of the town-gown relationships they are experiencing.

For instance, are campus and community partners working together in some locations of a municipality that are near the campus, but not others that are farther away? Relatedly, are some areas congested with projects, while others have been completely ignored? And what about centers, satellite campuses, and other college and university locations that are detached (and often quite far away) from the main campus? What is their relative impact on the perceptions of local residents? These are all testable questions that can be answered systematically with the OCTA tool.

The quantitative findings reported in chapter five also included a focus on a comparison and contrast of different combinations of campus and community roles. For example, the community stakeholders who reported the highest comfort levels with campus representatives were the business owners, followed by non-profit leaders, and then educators. While the educator comfort levels with Ohio State Mansfield representatives were still in relatively good shape, it still helped to know that increased activities

234

conducted with and for local school district personnel were important places to direct campus members' attention over time.

In contrast, if more extreme variations in subgroup perceptions are identified through the assessment process, this sort of information can become an important red flag regarding the need to more rapidly respond to such discrepant viewpoints within the community. As a result, these findings can serve as diagnostic information in terms of where to place one's immediate efforts to create more harmonious relationships.

This last point underscores the importance of gathering qualitative information alongside the more quantitatively oriented OCTA data. The themes derived from the open-ended questions posed in one pilot study (as reported in chapter five) were prescriptive in terms of what community members believed that campus representatives could do to improve town-gown relationships. In the best of all worlds, therefore, the qualitative and quantitative data are combined to create the fullest possible portrait of campus-community interaction. Not gathering a representative cross-section of community stakeholders creates the potential for unreliable results to be generated. Imagine how an overall portrait of a town-gown relationship might look if certain members of a particular stakeholder group – let's say for example, realtors who recently have been angered about a university decision to build more student housing on campus – did not participate in the survey.

It is imperative to systematically unpack findings and issues like this in light of the ninth commandment's aim to continually assess town-gown relationships. On this note, recall that data gathering was discussed in the sixth chapter as the "middle ground" of the Mobilization Cycle. This means that surveying efforts should be preceded by activities designed to obtain the highest quality data from respondents, and always followed by exercises intended to bring campus and community partners together in a data-informed manner.

Therefore, in a very real sense an adherence to the ninth commandment means that efforts within the Mobilization Cycle must be continuous in nature, and thus never really stop. More specifically, awareness raising and coalition building activities are always operational in a higher quality town-gown relationship. Recall the city manager who stated that "good town-gown relationships are bred out of persistence." Similarly, data interpretation and the creation and use of an evidence-based action plan also would seem to be consistent with the desire to be led continuously by the facts instead of gut feelings. Taken together, it is asserted here that harmonious relationships most credibly are built and maintained through a data-driven ideology.

Town-Gown Commandment #10: Thou shall leave the campus-community relationship in better shape than you found it.

Robert Stephenson Smyth Baden-Powell, the founder of the Boy Scouts, is quoted widely as having said that everyone should "try and leave this world a little better than you found it." As a result, the Boy Scouts developed a rule about their impact on the local environment: Always leave the campground a little cleaner than you found it. Borrowing from this canon of the outdoors, the tenth and final town-gown commandment strikes a similar pose: leave the campus and community a little better (i.e. a bit more harmonious) than you found it.

Truth be told, adherence to the tenth commandment is relatively easy if the first nine commandments have been followed. That said, one emerging trend that poses a potential threat to this commandment is the downward trajectory of time that college and university presidents are remaining in office. In 2006, the American Council on Education (ACE) reported that presidents had served an average of eight and a half years in their current positions. By 2012, that number had declined to seven years. While similar data were not available for city administrators, there has been a widespread belief that retirements are going to create large scale position vacancies in these management positions as well.

Any acceleration of turnover rates should be watched carefully, as the development and maintenance of personal associations among campus and community leaders plays such an important role in the long term health and well-being of town-gown relationships, as the entirety of this book attests. And even when campus and community leaders remain in their positions for longer periods of time, there is a pronounced need for succession planning that preserves the importance of town-gown relationships in the thoughts and actions of those who eventually will take over the helm.

Summary

The Ten Commandments of town-gown relationships were meant to serve as a series of statements about what campus and community leaders must do together as partners in order to build more harmonious relationships with one another. As noted in the first chapter of this book, these commandments were offered as a lighthearted set of instructions designed to provoke ongoing discussions about emerging best practices for university and municipal leaders.

These ten commandments can actually be broken into three subsets of directives. Taken together, the first four commandments serve as investment advice regarding the time and attention that campus and community leaders must give to building and sustaining their relationships with one another. Making town-gown relationships a high priority, setting aside the appropriate amount of time to nurture these associations, treating your partners with the utmost of respect, and seeking win-win outcomes wherever and whenever possible become the hallmarks of these relationship investment-oriented commandments.

The next three commandments focus on the central cast of characters that comprise the interface of campus and community. Institutions of higher learning exist for the primary purpose of educating students, and their students – for better and for worse – are the principal group that members of the community will interact with or otherwise get to know. Faculty members, in turn, are the individuals who are responsible for teaching those classes and conducting those research studies that provide the vehicles for students to gain their first entry points into the community. And of course those members of the community who are alumni of the college or university – and especially those who have risen to positions of leadership within the community – represent the group of citizens who have the greatest potential to impact the quality of the town-gown relationship.

The final three commandments focus attention on the past, present, and future of town-gown relationships. Those campus and community leaders who do not understand the history of campus-community interaction surely are doomed to repeat it. Likewise, those same leaders who are not using standardized measurement tools to assess the quality of their present town-gown relationships are destined to forever play a guessing game (and one that often as not will generate misleading information). And finally, the most effective university administrators and municipal authorities are those individuals who plan for a future that does not require their physical presence to maintain the work they have accomplished.

We shall end with a quote from Thomas Paine, who said that "when we are planning for posterity, we ought to remember that virtue is not hereditary." As applied to town-gown relationships, higher education and municipal leaders alike should not assume that future successors will automatically synchronize their goals and objectives to preserve and protect what has been accomplished already. Instead, these leaders must intentionally hardwire the prioritization of town-gown relationships into the organizational structure of the campus and community they have served.

REFERENCES

American Council on Education. *The American College President 2012.*

Washington, DC: American Council on Education, 2012.

Boszormenyi-Nagy, I., & Spark, G. (1973; 1984). *Invisible loyalties: Reciprocity*

in intergenerational family therapy. New York: Harper & Row.

Brockliss, L. (2000). Gown and town: The university and the city in Europe,

1200–2000. *Minerva, 38,* 147–170.

Bruning, S., McGrew, S., & Cooper, M. (2006). Town-gown relationships:

Exploring university-community engagement from the perspective

of community members. *Public Relations Preview, 32,* 125-130.

Crawford, M. 2014. A Century of Campus Planning: Past, Present, and

Future. *Planning for Higher Education,* 42 (3): 2-6.

Cooper, D. D. (1999). Academic professionalism and the betrayal of the

land-grant tradition. *American Behavioral Scientist, 42,* 776-785.

Cuber, J.F., & Harroff, P.B. (1965). *The significant Americans: A study of sexual*

behavior among the affluent. New York, NY: Appleton-Century-Crofts.

Day, R. D., Gavazzi, S. M., Miller, R., & van Langeveldt, A. (2009).

    Compelling family processes: Core constructs and key assumptions.

    Marriage and Family Review, 45, 116-128.

Fox, M. (2012). Challenges of the Town and Gown Relationship. *Municipal*

    World, September, *9*, 23-26.

Fox, M. (2014). *Town and gown: From conflict to cooperation.* Union, ON,

    Canada: Municipal World.

Gavazzi, S. M., (2015a). Engaged Institutions, Responsiveness, and Town-

    Gown Relationships: Why Deep Culture Change Must Emphasize

    the Gathering of Community Feedback. *Planning for Higher*

    Education, 43, 1-9.

Gavazzi, S. M., (2015b). For better and for worse: Understanding optimal

    campus-community relationships through the lens of marriage.

    Municipal Universities, 26, 147-154.

Gavazzi, S. M., (2015c). Using assessment methods to advance campus-to-

    campus and campus-community partnerships: Town-gown

    relationships as yours, mine, and ours. *Access: The Journal of the*

    National Association of Branch Campus Administrators, 1, 1-10.

Gavazzi, S. M., & Fox, M. (2015). A tale of three cities: Piloting a measure of effort and comfort levels within town-gown relationships. *Innovative Higher Education, 40,* 189-199.

Gavazzi, S. M., Fox, M., & Martin, J. (2014). Understanding campus and community relationships through marriage and family metaphors: A town-gown typology. *Innovative Higher Education, 39,* 361-374.

Gumprecht, B. (2008). *The American college town.* Amherst, MA: University of Massachusetts Press.

Kellogg Commission on the Future of State and Land-Grant Universities (2000). *Returning to our Roots: Executive Summaries of the Reports of the Kellogg Commission on the Future of State and Land-Grant Universities.* Washington, DC: National Association of State Universities and Land-Grant Colleges.

Kemp, R. L. (2013). *Town and gown relations: A handbook of best practices.* Jefferson, NC: McFarland.

McGirr, D., Kull, R., & Enns, K. S. (2003). Town and gown. *Economic Development Journal, 2,* 16–23.

Lawrence, F. L. (2006). *Leadership in higher education: Views from the presidency.* New Brunswick, NJ: Transaction Publishers.

Optimal College Town Assessment (OCTA).

    http://www.collegetownassessment.com

Pierce, S. R. (2012). *On Being Presidential: A Guide for College and University*

    Leaders. San Francisco: Wiley and Sons.

Porter, M., & Grogan, P. (2013). Urban renewal. In *Town and gown relations:*

    A handbook of best practices, R. L. Kemp (ed.), pp. 223-227. Jefferson,

    North Carolina: McFarland.

Smith, D. (2008). The politics of studentification and (un)balanced urban

    populations: lessons for gentrification and sustainable

    communities? *Urban Studies, 12*, 2541-2564.

Sungi-Eryilmaz, Y. (2009). *Town-gown collaboration in land use and development*.

    Cambridge, MA: Lincoln Institute of Land Policy.

Weill, L. V. 2009. The President's Role in Cultivating Positive Town-

    Gown Relationships. *Planning for Higher Education*, 37 (4): 37-

    42.

Zehr, H. 2002. *The Little Book of Restorative Justice*, Intercourse, PA: Good

    Books.

ABOUT THE AUTHOR

Stephen M. Gavazzi , Ph.D. is Dean and Director of The Ohio State University at Mansfield regional campus, and is a Professor in the Department of Human Sciences in the College of Education and Human Ecology on the Columbus campus. He is a trained family therapist whose scholarship for the past thirty years has surrounded the impact that family dynamics have on adolescent development and behavior. He has written a book for parents of teenagers entitled *"Strong Families, Successful Students"* that was published in 2010, and a classroom textbook entitled *"Families with Adolescents: Bridging the Gaps Between Theory, Research, and Practice"* that was published in 2011 by Springer Press.

Professor Gavazzi's most recent scholarship centers on the establishment and maintenance of healthy campus-community relationships. His work on town-gown issues makes ample use of his marriage and family therapy background, drawing parallels between campus-community relationships and marriages. This work is examined in detail in his most recent book, *The Optimal Town-Gown Marriage: Taking Campus-Community Outreach and Engagement to the Next Level,* providing readers with a conceptual framework and standardized assessment tools that are designed to more systematically understand and measure campus-community interaction.

57717783R00142

Made in the USA
Lexington, KY
22 November 2016